NOT
Accountable

Rethinking the

Constitutionality of

Public Employee Unions

PHILIP K. HOWARD

**RODIN
BOOKS**™

RODIN
BOOKS™

ISBN 978-1-957588-12-4
PUBLISHED BY RODIN BOOKS INC.
666 Old Country Road, Suite 510
Garden City, New York 11530

www.rodinbooks.com

Book and cover design by Alexia Garaventa

Manufactured in the United States of America

To Tony Kiser and Scott Smith

Contents

Foreword
by Mitch Daniels

When will America start listening to Philip Howard? For every citizen driven to distraction (and who isn't?) by the waste, slowness, and sheer maddening incompetence of government, Howard has been offering well-documented explanations for more than a quarter century. How does an agency decide that sand is a poison? How in the world can it take forty-seven permits, by nineteen agencies over almost five years, doubling the cost in the process, to add a couple new lanes to a bridge that is already there? Howard has been providing the diagnoses and practical prescriptions, but the patient is stubbornly noncompliant.

In *The Death of Common Sense*, and its equally insightful and appalling sequel, *The Rule of Nobody*, Howard dissected the public sector's inability to get anything done at any reasonable cost in any reasonable amount of time and exposed the way that ever-accreting rules have replaced human judgment and accountability. By sliding into "governing by excruciating detail," he demonstrated, we have given ourselves "the worst of both worlds, regulation that goes too far while it does too little... How we do things has become more important than what is done."

Then, in *Life Without Lawyers*, came example after example of the way a "government of laws, not of men" became a "government of laws against men." Why, for example, are public school teachers rendered impotent to maintain even basic order in their classrooms, or businesses to give honest job references? In a society where lawsuits, or just the threat of them, paralyze decision-making and intimidate bureaucrats out of even the simplest trade-offs, someone inevitably will "press the risk button and discussion pretty much ends."

The recent bipartisan infrastructure law includes Howard's reforms capping the size of reviews and limiting permitting time to two years. But that success, dispiritingly, is an anomaly. His "spring housecleaning" of obsolete laws and counterproductive regulations would make a huge difference in any jurisdiction that takes it seriously.

But after a couple decades appealing with limited success to public officials and those who elect them, he has come—reluctantly I'm sure—to the conclusion that the system cannot be fixed through the ballot box. Our governments have become "impervious to reform" because "elected officials no longer have effective authority over the operations of government."

So he's gone to, as the social scientists like to say, the "root cause." To Howard, this means the control of government that public employee unions have seized and wielded not merely to plunder treasuries and to dictate the actions—most often, the inactions—of government at all levels, but simultaneously to control the elections through which reform could theoretically occur. This time, he proposes a fix that this most powerful of special interests cannot block with campaign contributions.

Calling on the deep legal knowledge that took him to the top of his profession, the author crafts a strong case that the lurch into public unionization, dismissed as unthinkable by such labor champions as Franklin Roosevelt and George Meany, was not only misguided but unconstitutional. His multilayered indictment challenges both the executive branch's delegation of its authority to run the government and the Congress's legal power to ratify that delegation.

In what must be the most ironic, and most historically demolished, words ever written in a presidential executive order, President Kennedy's EO 10988 stated the aim of promoting "the efficient administration of the Government" and the "effective conduct of public business." Its subsequent cascade through all levels of government has delivered the opposite of these goals to an extent that is comical until one contemplates the damage it does daily.

In the days before commencing my one stint in elected office, I struggled with one decision above all the others then pending: whether to strike down Indiana's long-standing collective bargaining agreement with state employees. Unlike in most jurisdictions, Indiana's

General Assembly had never codified the practice in statute, so the choice was mine to make.

I tried to justify postponing the call, or splitting the difference somehow, out of concern that a huge reform agenda on which we had sought office might be jeopardized by a union-led uproar. But ultimately I concluded that the myriad changes we hoped to bring to a broke and broken state government could not be achieved if every step could become the subject of a rules-laden negotiation under a 170-page collective bargaining agreement.

I may have faced more difficult decisions but probably never a more consequential one. After eight years with the freedom to recruit and place top talent in key jobs, separate some agencies for priority attention while consolidating or abolishing others, and reward employees for their performance rather than their seniority, government became not just solvent but effective. Tax refunds were received in two weeks or less, citizens were in and out of a motor vehicle license branch in twelve minutes or less, and a national survey found 77 percent confidence in the job Indiana state government was doing.

Ultimately, this is the goal to which Philip Howard has committed so much thought and effort. He seeks to reform dysfunctional government not just for efficiency's sake but for democracy's, because government of the people depends crucially on the people's confidence, and endless ineptness destroys that confidence.

If Mr. Howard is correct, America does not need an aroused majority of millions to redress the corruption of our free institutions, only a judicial system willing to examine fairly the arguments of this learned fellow attorney and purely motivated public citizen. Let's all hope Philip Howard gets his day, which would be a great day for all Americans, in court.

Introduction

Derek Chauvin, the policeman who killed George Floyd in Minneapolis in 2020, had a history of citizen complaints and was thought to be "tightly wound," not a trait ideal for someone patrolling the streets with a deadly weapon. But under the police union's collective bargaining agreement, the police commissioner lacked the authority to dismiss Derek Chauvin, or even to reassign him. The lack of supervisory authority resulted in harms that continue to reverberate in American society.

No society, no organization, no group of people, can function effectively without accountability. Accountability is essential for mutual trust. The prospect of accountability is the backdrop for a culture of shared energy and values. "A social organism of any sort whatever, large or small, is what it is because each member proceeds to his own duty," philosopher William James noted, "with a trust that the other members will simultaneously do theirs."

The absence of accountability, by contrast, is a recipe for a cynical and ineffective organization. Why do what's right, or go the extra mile, when you know performance doesn't matter? Distrust corrodes daily dealings. The broad sense that bad cops get away with abusive conduct helped fuel the national protests after the killing of George Floyd.

Accountability is basically nonexistent in American government. Performance doesn't matter. Many public managers tell me they've never seen a public employee dismissed for poor performance. The Minneapolis police department had received twenty-six hundred complaints in the decade prior to 2020. Twelve led to discipline, of which the most severe was a forty-hour suspension. Blatant misconduct is just the starting point for a negotiation. In 2019, a school principal in New York was discovered to have created a fraudulent system of school achievement. His penalty? He lost his position, but, because of public employee protections, he will get full salary and benefits of over $265,000 annually for the next seven years. An EPA employee, caught red-handed surfing porn sites in his cubicle, was paid for almost two years until he made a deal to retire.

The lack of accountability isn't a secret, of course. Nor is the reason. Police unions, teachers unions, and other public sector unions have built a fortress against supervisory decisions. Political observers rue union power but treat it as a state of nature. No matter who is elected, no matter what their party, they hit a brick wall of union resistance. California governors Jerry Brown and Arnold Schwarzenegger, Chicago mayors Rahm Emanuel and Lori Lightfoot, New York mayors Ed Koch and Mike Bloomberg—they all crashed into the union wall.

Lack of accountability, however, is only the tip of the union iceberg. Almost without anyone noticing how it happened, public employee unions have taken a tight grip on the daily operations of government. While headlines from Washington and state capitols focus on policy initiatives, say, dealing with COVID or climate change, the operating machinery of government grinds along at half capacity or less. No decision is too small to be vetoed by a union entitlement. A New York City Parks Department employee filed a grievance against a supervisor who asked him to straighten his nameplate. The worker argued that the supervisor had made an "inappropriate unannounced visit."

The harms of unmanageable government ripple through every part of society. The resulting inefficiency basically burns taxpayer money. David Osborne and Ted Gaebler in *Reinventing Government* reported that "on average public service delivery is 35 to 95 percent more expensive than contracting" out the services to a private firm. Rigid job categories substantially raise maintenance costs at New York's Metropolitan Transportation Authority; a worker doing signal repair is not allowed, for example, to cut an overhead branch. The size of work crews is bloated by the need to assign workers for each job category even if that part of the work is incidental.

Governing is not just about money. Government provides essential services that, in many ways, influence our culture and future. None is more important than schools. But decades of reforms have done little to fix the bleak performance of many school districts. After Hurricane Katrina forced the closing of schools in New Orleans, however, the public school system was replaced by independent charter schools no longer subject to teachers union collective bargaining agreements. The differences were transformative. It was as if someone switched on the light. High school graduation rates improved from 52 to 72 percent, and gaps between racial groups narrowed.

About twenty-two million people work for government in America, two-thirds at the local level, as cops, teachers, inspectors, sanitation workers, social workers, highway crews, and many others doing essential tasks. Most federal programs are implemented by state and local employees. Overwhelmingly, studies and stories suggest, these public employees want to do what's right. But many, perhaps most, are stuck in public work cultures that bring out the worst in people. It's dispiriting to work in a setting where people focus on entitlements instead of pride in accomplishment. In *Government Against Itself*, political scientist Daniel DiSalvo tells the story of a female painter from the Facilities Department at City College of New York who, having seen DiSalvo talk about union rules on television, stopped by on her coffee break:

> In her late 40s with a strong Queens accent, dressed in a white t-shirt and white painters' pants, she was clearly a strong woman who had worked hard in a profession dominated by men. She told me that she'd been working at CCNY for

about a year—mostly, she said, because of the attractive pension and health benefits. But she hated it. She couldn't believe how much time it took to do anything. She couldn't believe what people were paid for what little work, in her telling, that they did. ... She couldn't stand the detailed rules. She felt insulted because they didn't allow her to prove how fast and how talented a painter she was. The combination of unionization and government employment was undermining her pride in her craft. And she worried that the poor upkeep of many buildings was a disservice to the lower-income, immigrant, and first-generation college students ...

Something is terribly amiss in a public culture where good people can't do their best. I've studied government for more than twenty-five years, and the more I look into the causes of public failure and frustration, the clearer I see that the only path out is to liberate people to act on their best judgment. Give people responsibility and give other people the responsibility to oversee them. That's the basic framework of the Constitution—allocating powers among different officials and branches.

Political candidates often call for a return to responsibility. But it doesn't happen. That's largely because public employee unions in most jurisdictions have a veto on key aspects of how government works. The federal government and thirty-eight states have authorized in some form collective bargaining—giving unions the exclusive right to represent public employees. In most of the remaining states, public employee unions have consolidated sufficient political power to block or influence reforms they don't like. The banner that flies over the union fortress reads "Just Say No." Elected leaders come and go, but public unions just say no.

The veto power of public unions comes from an arsenal of legal rights that were acquired and are enforced by hard-knuckle political power. In 1979, the New Jersey teachers union demonstrated its ability to organize the defeat of politicians who disagreed with union positions. Democratic Assemblyman Daniel Newman, the Education Committee chair and "one of the most powerful figures in New Jersey education," opposed increasing state aid to schools and giving teachers the right to strike. The state union, with help from the national union, mobilized an anti-Newman campaign that led to his defeat in the next election. The message was not lost on other legislators: "As a result of my experience," Newman noted, "legislators are scared of the teachers groups."

Public union power is not the focus of continual exposés and scandal probably because, at this point, almost everyone takes for granted the preemptive union position and the resulting public inefficiencies and idiocies. But the abuse of power by public employee unions is the main story of public failure in America—worse even, I believe, than polarization or red tape. It is not possible to bring purpose and hope back to political discourse until, as a threshold condition, elected leaders regain the authority to run public operations.

Unlike my previous books, this is not a story of a flawed governing philosophy applied by people acting in good faith. This is a story of raw power and democratic disloyalty.

In this book, I describe the sources of power and how public employee unions came to acquire it, and how unions have corroded democratic governance. The cure I describe is not political but constitutional. The disempowerment of democratically elected officials, and the conflict of interest by public employees mobilizing against the public good, undermine core principles of the Constitution.

SECTION I:
Unions Against Democracy

Chapter 1:
Why Nothing Much Gets Fixed

"Governments … deriv[e] their just powers
from the consent of the governed."

—The Declaration of Independence

Bad schools, unaccountable police, and other endemic failures of modern American government share one defining trait: They are impervious to reform. No matter who is elected, no matter the voter demand for change, government almost never changes how it works. It can add new programs, but periodic reform attempts in schools and other areas generate noise without results. Government grinds slowly toward the future like a huge robot, programmed decades ago to do things one way.

The effects are predictable: growing citizen frustration and anger; broad distrust of police and other governing institutions; students ill educated to compete and even to be self-sufficient; and stupendous public inefficiency and waste. Some states are insolvent, unable to meet their future obligations.

Running decent schools should not be the great challenge of our time. Nor should terminating a cop with a hair-trigger temper, or cutting fat from bloated public programs. Every election, American voters elect new leaders who promise to do these things.

They all fail, for one main reason: Elected executives—the president, governors, and mayors—no longer have effective authority over the operations of government. Nor do their appointees. Nor do public supervisors, such as school principals, police captains, and crew chiefs on highway repair teams.

Over the past five decades, starting with the legalization of public collective bargaining in the 1960s, public employee unions have progressively imposed restrictions on public managers. Collective bargaining agreements effectively bar the most important management tool—accountability. They also preclude basic management choices—including reassigning personnel and allocating responsibilities for projects. They restrict mundane managerial prerogatives, such as dropping in on a classroom or asking people how to improve things.

The plague of public powerlessness has other sources as well. Another governing change coming out of the 1960s was to prescribe one correct way to do things—resulting in thousand-page rule books. Instead of a simple framework of understandable goals and principles, law became a micromanagement headache for officials as well as citizens. To top it off, an expanded idea of individual rights allowed any disgruntled person to throw a monkey wrench into any decision he or she didn't like.

Micromanagement and expansive rights also became integral to the public union playbook for control—no innovation is allowed unless the official can show it complies with a rule; no decision about a public employee's performance is valid without objective proof in a trial-type hearing. Clearing out this legal underbrush is what's needed to restore officials' freedom to use common sense in daily choices. But that can never happen unless officials can be accountable when they abuse the privilege. The public employee unions won't budge.

The harm to the common good caused by all these restrictions is irrefutable: Government is failing in core responsibilities. No plausible public purpose is served by restrictive union micromanagement. Nor is there any public purpose for abusive fiscal entitlements in public union contracts—including overstaffing, massive overtime for minor schedule changes, and pensions "spiked" by rigged overtime in the last year of work. Government can't possibly deliver what taxpayers deserve until elected executives are re-empowered to make basic management decisions. But public employee unions block the door to a better government, arms crossed.

Reading through the catalogs of union restrictions and entitlements, it seems that unions must have extortive power. How else could they secure restrictions and benefits so one-sided and harmful to the public interest? In fact, public employee unions do have extortive power. For starters, government can't work without public employees. Government is not like a factory that can be moved elsewhere when labor demands are unreasonable. Also, unlike trade union negotiations, public employee unions have little downside risk with excessive collective bargaining demands—no matter how much unions take from taxpayers and the public good, government can't go out of business. Nor is there any other organized opposing force—just the broad interests of the public good.

Against this backdrop of little resistance, public employee unions have become the elephant in the room of American politics—one of the largest campaign contributors, and also the largest source of campaign workers. All this political power is consolidated toward one goal—protecting and benefiting public employees against decisions by elected officials and public supervisors. For five decades since the 1960s, public employee unions have flexed their political muscles to control government operations through statutes and collective bargaining agreements.

Political leaders sometimes try to cajole or entice unions into lifting the most onerous restrictions, with occasional marginal movement. But only a few officials have been willing to endure a holy war with public unions. Even reformers try to work around the elephant instead of pushing it out of daily operations. What else can they do? Mobilizing the political will to clean out decades of union entitlements is so unrealistic that no party has that platform.

But unions have gone too far. All these controls and restrictions have disabled basic principles of constitutional government. Executive branch officials no longer have the authority needed to fulfill their democratic responsibilities. Eliminating accountability and supervisory judgment removed the main tools of public managers. What is left are facades of governing institutions without the activating powers for executive officials to make things work.

In our constitutional republic, legislatures are not authorized to pass laws that gut executive power. Nor do governors and mayors have authority to abdicate or delegate their executive power, even when they want to for political gain. A core constitutional principle applicable to both federal and state government is the "nondelegation doctrine," which protects state sovereignty by preventing delegation of core responsibilities to private groups. Specific provisions of the Constitution are also violated by statutes that mandate collective bargaining and cede management controls to public unions:

(i) The executive branch must regain power to provide public services effectively and implement legislative goals. The structure of American government, reflected in the federal as well as almost every state constitution, divides the power into executive, legislative, and judicial branches. For federal government, a long line of Supreme Court precedent interprets the scope of "executive Power," and makes clear that Congress cannot, for example, take away the president's "exclusive and illimitable power of removal" of executive officials. Statutes that remove the authority to hold public employees accountable, and that restrict executive prerogatives by requiring collective bargaining agreements, unconstitutionally restrict executive authority.

(ii) The Constitution requires that state and local elected officials retain the authority needed to fulfill their governing responsibilities. While there is judicial disagreement over whether courts should enforce it, the Guarantee Clause in Article IV provides that states must have "a Republican Form of Government"—requiring governing power to be exercised by officials who are accountable to voters. Giving governing controls to any "favored class" is a violation of the Guarantee Clause.

(iii) Public employee political activity raises constitutional issues of first impression regarding the conflict between union political activity and the fiduciary duties of public employees. Unlike other politically active interest groups, public employees occupy a position of public trust. Their fiduciary duty stands in direct conflict with organized union political activity aimed at securing legal powers and benefits that undermine constitutional governance. In upholding restrictions on federal employee political activity fifty years ago, the Supreme Court cautioned "that the rapidly expanding Government workforce should not be employed to build a powerful, invincible, and perhaps corrupt political machine." Those fears have been realized. The conflict of interest by public employees in negotiating against government is notorious and unavoidable and requires a constitutional bright-line test against public sector union political activity.

At this point, five decades into the age of public union power, public employee unions consider all these legal controls and restrictions their entitlement. Public unions will note that all these restrictions have been approved by legislatures and elected officials, using democratic processes. But those approvals can't rescue the constitutional defect: the preemption of essential executive powers. Nor does continued legislative acquiescence, in the face of union political power, in any way mitigate the unconstitutional harms to government and to society as a whole.

The operating machinery of American democracy is now in the grips of public unions. Voters elect officials who have been disempowered by union controls. Problems don't get fixed. Bad public employees can't be fired. Public resources are squandered. Leadership has turned into finger-pointing. Extremism flourishes as institutions flail. Citizens are justifiably cynical and distrustful, because modern government is organized to fail.

Chapter 2:
How Public Employee Unions Seized Control of Public Administration

"How can one expect rational administration when good men are held in the same esteem as bad ones?"

—Polybius

Public union power is basically a creature of the 1960s rights revolution. But there was no scandal or moral awakening that prompted collective bargaining. To the contrary, a report by New Dealer Jim Landis to President-elect JFK concluded that the administrative flaw in postwar government was sluggishness—federal employees were, basically, fat and happy. Civil service systems regularized pay and personnel procedures. State and local governments were no better or worse than the people and the mores in those communities. But public union leaders had been angling for bargaining power for decades, and the strong incoming tide of individual rights provided cover for the unions' political patrons to enact laws claiming to protect the rights of public employees.

Until the rights revolution in the 1960s, the idea of negotiating against the public interest was unthinkable. AFL-CIO president George Meany in 1955 stated bluntly that it is "impossible to bargain collectively with the Government." Negotiating against government was also considered antisocial and fraught with political dangers. Public employee unions with bargaining power would hold vastly more power over government than private unions over business—they not only would constitute a huge political bloc, but they would hold the authority of the state in their hands, without having to honor market realities of affordability and efficiency. FDR could hardly have been firmer:

> Meticulous attention should be paid to the special relationships and obligations of public servants to the public itself and to the Government ... The process of collective bargaining, as usually understood, cannot be transplanted into the public service.

But public employees had the makings of a powerful political force. Civil service reforms in the Progressive Era— replacing the spoils system in which public jobs turned over with each change of the party in power—had given public jobs a permanence that naturally organized into a voting bloc. Ending the spoils systems, political scientist Daniel DiSalvo explains, also left a political vacuum. With civil service, party bosses had less ability to distribute public jobs as favors. So where would political parties look for campaign workers and contributions?

Growing advocacy by public workers led Teddy Roosevelt in 1902 to impose a gag rule, not rescinded for a decade, barring federal workers and postal workers from lobbying Congress. Congress was sufficiently alarmed by political activities of public employees in the 1936 election that it enacted the Hatch Act in 1939 barring "political activity" by federal employees.

Political leaders after World War II who wanted to free themselves from the remaining grip of party bosses saw organized public employees as a preferable alternative. The first shoe to drop was New York City, where Mayor Robert Wagner decided to "break the back of the Tammany Hall political machine," according to DiSalvo, by authorizing collective bargaining by executive order in 1958. Wisconsin authorized collective bargaining in 1959.

The big break came with JFK's Executive Order 10988 in 1962, authorizing collective bargaining in the federal government. The order stated that its aim was to promote the "efficient administration of the Government" and "effective conduct of public business." But the actual motivation was political, and historians have concluded that the Executive Order 10988 was payback for union support.

Even without collective bargaining, the growth of big government gave public employees political power. The activism of the 1960s inspired public workers to take matters into their own hands. National headlines were made by strikes by teachers in Utah, by social workers and then transit workers in New York City, and by Detroit police suffering from "blue flu." Avoiding future strife with public employees was another motivation for authorizing collective bargaining.

New York State authorized public collective bargaining in 1967. The independent Taylor Committee in 1966, concerned about preserving democratic accountability to voters, recommended that the legislature should approve each new collective bargaining agreement. But the New York legislature brushed away worries about unions seizing management control or skewing democratic priorities. Other states soon followed with generally similar statutes—over twenty states, including California, by the end of 1968.

The ostensible quid pro quo was that public unions would not strike, but many states already banned strikes, and the second Taylor Committee in 1968 concluded that the ban on strikes was largely toothless. "The only illegal strike," as one union leader put it, "is an unsuccessful strike." When approving collective bargaining, thirteen states did not even bother to require that unions in their agreements agree not to strike. One of the last states to authorize collective bargaining was Illinois, in 1983, because Chicago mayor Richard Daley did not want to relinquish the power of his political machine. Southern states and a few mountain states, generally hostile to organized labor, did not go along.

Ultimately thirty-eight states authorized collective bargaining—twenty-five (including the District of Columbia) with broad authorization across many classes of public employees, and thirteen that limited bargaining to specific job categories, such as police or teachers, or limited the scope of bargaining to compensation issues. In most of the remaining states, unions developed leverage through weaker "meet and confer" requirements and through organized political activity. The federal government authorized bargaining over work conditions and discipline but not compensation and benefits, which are set by civil service schedules.

By 1980, public employee unions had burgeoned to a size that made them a predominant political player in many states. Today, membership is about seven million active public employees. The two teachers unions (the National Education Association and the American Federation of Teachers) have about 4.6 million members, including retirees. Other public unions include the American Federation of State, County and Municipal Employees (AFSCME) with roughly 1.3 million members; the Service Employees International Union (SEIU), which represents roughly one million public employees; the Fraternal Order of Police, with 357,000 members; the American Federation of Government Employees (AFGE), with 300,000 members; and the National Treasury Employees Union (NTEU), with 80,000 members.

Overall, 35 percent of public employees in America belong to unions: 25 percent in federal government, 30 percent in state government, and 40 percent in local government. In states that mandate collective bargaining, the concentration is much higher: half to two-thirds of all public employees in California, Connecticut, Illinois, Minnesota, New Jersey, New York, Oregon, Pennsylvania, and Rhode Island belong to unions.

Public sector collective bargaining laws were generally modeled on the National Labor Relations Act of 1935, which gave exclusive bargaining rights to private sector trade unions with the vote of over half the workers. But the analogy to private sector bargaining was only skin-deep, and public sector unions soon set out to do what is impossible in the private sector—to "capture" the officials on the other side of the table.

Bargaining over Public Choices Is a Recipe for Collusion, not Good Government

Proponents of public-sector bargaining had the notion they were just equalizing the rights of public employees and private employees. As one observer concluded, it's "difficult to make ... a case for depriving [public employees] of the right to bargain where a majority so desires."

But there are "salient differences" between trade union and public sector bargaining. "In private employment collective bargaining is a process ... shaped primarily by market forces," labor law expert Clyde Summers explained, "while in public employment it is a process of governmental decision-making shaped ultimately by political forces."

What that means, translated into realpolitik, is that unions in the public sector can get what they want by helping friendly politicians get elected. As labor leader Victor Gotbaum put it, "We have the ability, in a sense, to elect our own boss." Public sector "bargaining" is a misnomer; the process is more like a transaction: benefits at the bargaining table in exchange for campaign support.

This back-scratching arrangement reaps far more than other political interest group alliances because collective bargaining gives the union exclusive representation rights. Management must make a deal with the union, one way or the other. Even today, however, many experts don't fully appreciate why public sector bargaining is different. Leaving aside the common goal of fair pay, almost nothing about private and public bargaining is the same.

Trade union bargaining

The origin story for private sector bargaining arose out of abusive business behavior in the late nineteenth century—unsafe and mean practices by manufacturers, exposed in books such as Upton Sinclair's *The Jungle*. Allowing employees to unionize created a counterbalance against profit-maximizing capitalists both as to working conditions and for an equitable split of the economic benefits. For decades these conflicting interests led to violence and illegal activity by both sides. Eventually something like an equilibrium was reached, basic rules for negotiating were set out in the NLRA in 1935, and trade unions for a time became dominant in large industries such as steel, autos, and textiles.

Today, only about 6 percent of the private workforce belongs to trade unions, down from a high of about 35 percent in the 1950s. The decline has many causes, including the loss of manufacturing jobs to overseas competitors (in part due to high costs of union labor), the growth of service industries (where jobs are less standardized), and less need for health and safety protections as a result of regulation. Trade unions in America are largely now confined to large manufacturers in the Rust Belt and to construction trades.

Trade union negotiations basically divide the pie of profit between capital and labor. Bargaining is constrained by the distinct economic risks on each side. Demanding too much may cause the business to close or move to other states or overseas. Demands that reduce profit—for example, with inefficient work rules—may also be counterproductive, because they leave less profit to divvy up. Trade unions learned this the hard way by overbearing demands on car makers and other industrial companies in the 1960s and 1970s, which had the effect of driving jobs elsewhere.

Aside from basic principles of fair dealing, labor law generally leaves the union and company free to reach a bargain, or not. One clear legal prohibition is that management can't be on both sides of the table—for example, helping friendly workers organize a compliant union. Without a legal ban, the opportunities for collusion and corruption are too great.

Even with reduced market penetration, the presence of trade unions, many observers believe, provides a frame of reference for fair dealing across the industries. The continued presence of auto unions puts pressure on nonunion domestic auto makers to provide comparable benefits and protections.

Public sector bargaining

For decades during the apex of unionization in industry, the reasons not to allow public sector bargaining were well understood. Bargaining against the common good was a conflict of interest. Nor was there the imperative to deal with abusive and dangerous work conditions. Public employees had long enjoyed civil service protections, providing for equal pay schedules and fair treatment.

The differences between public and private bargaining are differences in kind, not degree. Government bargaining has few market constraints. Government can't go out of business, so unions can demand ever more—a kind of one-way ratchet that never stops raising public costs. Where industry sees inefficiencies as a deal killer, many politicians readily accede to inefficiencies as a way to benefit public employees. The more jobs, the better. How these agreements affect government effectiveness, moreover, is difficult to measure. Because government isn't run for profit and has nothing like quarterly earnings reports, it's hard for the public to see profligate spending and inefficiencies.

The general indifference to inefficiency in public bargaining impacts not only the cost of government but also the delivery of public services. Public unions have made rigid management controls into a kind of entitlement—strict seniority and supervisory restrictions are union "accomplishments." Most unionized businesses, by contrast, would never accept deliberate inefficiencies and rigidities. They could not long stay in business by delivering mediocre products and services at a high price.

Because government generally allocates a fixed budget, social interests not at the bargaining table inevitably get the short end of the stick. Should the school budget fund a long-planned vocational training program, or should the program be shut down so that teachers get a salary increase? In that situation, which arose as soon as collective bargaining was authorized in Michigan, the vocational program was abandoned because the teachers exercised their bargaining power to get the raise. Public sector bargaining thus partially preempts the responsibility of officials to make trade-offs among competing public goods.

The most important distinction between public and private bargaining, as noted, is that public management is responsive to political inducements, not the marketplace. Instead of bargaining over the split of economic gain, the parties are seeking different benefits altogether—public officials want political support, and unions want employee entitlements. Instead of dividing the pie, they offer each other inducements. What makes this negotiation collusive is that they're negotiating with the public's money for their parochial benefits. Labor lawyer Theodore Clark early on diagnosed the conceptual flaw: "Collective bargaining is premised on … two parties which are essentially in adversarial roles" where "neither party should be able to interfere with the other party's bargaining representatives." "The political aspects of public sector collective bargaining," Clark concluded, "jeopardize the very premise on which collective bargaining exists."

Payoffs that would be unlawful in business bargaining have become a common feature of public bargaining—unions are making massive campaign donations to the politicians with whom they will then be negotiating. It's a point of pride—the unions brandish their political power like a sword. The head of a federal employee union in 2015 bragged that "we are a force to be reckoned with" and any "fools" in Congress who vote against union interests will find that the unions "will open up the biggest can of whoop ass on anyone." A 2010 video in the California legislative chamber showed an SEIU official telling a group of legislators, "We helped to get you into office, and we got a good memory ... Come November, if you don't back our program, we'll get you out of office."

By making politicians dependent on their support, as Clark predicted, unions, "in effect, sit on both sides of the bargaining table." In 2006, an "impassioned" New Jersey governor Jon Corzine "spoke to a Trenton rally of roughly 10,000 public workers and shouted out: 'We will fight for a fair contract!'" But Governor Corzine was management—Whom was he going to fight?

Put yourself in the shoes of an elected executive with a limited budget. How do you govern sensibly when a long line of union officials are waiting with their demands? You will have a hard discussion, especially if you are dependent on union political support. Now consider that you have a legal obligation under collective bargaining laws to, in effect, satisfy the unions. In some jurisdictions that obligation is backed by compulsory arbitration or by a continuation of the collective bargaining agreement until there's a new agreement. Now consider that part of the contract is to allow union reps, in many corners of government, to challenge daily supervisory decisions.

Democracy can't devote itself to the common good when the first challenge is to satisfy the union. "In order for an institution to be a *government*," Professor Sylvester Petro explained in a long essay about public sector bargaining, "it needs to have undivided and unchallengeable power to perform the functions it assumes."

Writing in 1974, Petro concluded that there is an "irreconcilable conflict between meaningful sovereign government and meaningful public-sector collective bargaining." The constitutional defect has been there since the outset, and experience at all levels of government since then has confirmed that the flaws are inherent in the experiment. Even Petro and Clark, however, did not predict the extent to which public unions would infiltrate the operating machinery of government.

Government by the Unions, for the Unions

American government changed almost immediately when collective bargaining was enacted. Public unions lined up and, as one observer put it, "plunged into municipal treasuries like a starved man whose only thought is to eat as much as he can swallow." As I will shortly describe in more detail, in many jurisdictions, almost every aspect of public operations, including mundane managerial choices, became subject to union veto:

—Accountability became virtually impossible. Public supervisors could terminate no public employee without enduring a gauntlet of procedures, consuming several years of managerial time, with the burden of proof on supervisors. As a practical matter, except for lewd or criminal conduct, almost no public employee can be dismissed without a massive managerial commitment, and even then the chance of success is low. California, with 300,000 teachers, is able to terminate two or three per year for poor performance.

—Work rules became an exercise in micromanagement. For promotions, reassignments, and layoffs, employee seniority trumped supervisors' judgments about job performance. Detailed job descriptions provided the logic for a byzantine structure for overstaffing and make-work.

Asking an employee to help out was often barred, or it became a basis for a day's extra pay. Overtime kicked in on longer shifts even when the employee only worked forty hours in a week. Reassignment was impossible except by going through a legal process. Daily decisions had to be negotiated with the on-site union representative. Any workplace dispute had to ultimately be resolved by arbitrators who were approved by the unions.

—Public benefits became progressively richer: many public employees could retire after twenty or thirty years—in their forties and fifties—with full benefits. Pensions could be inflated by up to double or more by "spiking" overtime in the last year. Unrealistic assumptions of a guaranteed rate of return allowed unions to avoid reasonable reserves for these rich pensions and thereby preserve current spending. Health benefits were gold-plated and did not require the usual employee contributions.

—Public inefficiency dragged down the broader economy. "Unlike unions in the private sector," Professor DiSalvo observes, "government unions have incentives to push for more public employment, which increases their ranks, fills their coffers with new dues, and makes them more powerful. Therefore, they consistently push for higher taxes and more government activity. Over the long term, this can stifle economic growth and pit public and private sector unions against each other."

The shopping spree by unions reflects the unprecedented political war chest that public employee unions amassed with the exclusive rights afforded by collective bargaining. Annual union revenues from dues are on the order of $5 billion. Much of this is spent on direct and indirect political activity. Public employee unions are a powerful force in national politics and by far the dominant force in state and local politics where collective bargaining is authorized.

In addition to campaign contributions, public unions mobilize thousands of members as campaign workers, including staffing candidates' campaign offices. They also run members as candidates, for example, to local school boards. The unions are structured as national federations with local branches, so that resources from one state can be used to snuff out reforms in other states. The political resources of public unions enable them to exercise influence even in states, such as Georgia and Arizona, that do not authorize collective bargaining. Any reform initiative is also discouraged by the background threat of job actions, and the up-front threat of political retribution.

Public employee unions are not only different from trade unions, but they are also different in kind than other interest groups. The jostling at the public trough by myriad outside interest groups involves straightforward trade-offs: Do we give public resources to this group or that? But public sector unions are not merely competing for government favors but, uniquely, have the legal right to bargain over how government works. These controls are embedded in a web of statutory restrictions woven ever thicker since the 1960s. Each new statutory mandate and entitlement further insulates public employees from reform.

Democratic processes cannot solve this problem. Reform-minded governors and mayors have been disempowered by collective bargaining agreements and statutory restrictions and no longer have effective operating authority. Negotiating better collective bargaining agreements at the end of their term is also precluded, in many jurisdictions, by statutes that require any stalemate to be resolved by arbitrators. Who elected them?

A wholesale replacement of legislators is theoretically possible, but no existing party has ever thought this would work. Citizens could organize a new movement and go to the barricades, but it's hard to imagine an impassioned movement with banners like "Public Administration for the People." Those goals are supposed to be subsumed within the responsibility of any president, governor, or mayor, not require a democratic uprising. Opposing any overhaul effort to remove decades of statutes and collective bargaining rights, the public unions would call upon billions of campaign funds, existing political alliances, hordes of campaign workers, and threats of shutting down government.

A political path toward responsible government operations is, realistically, impossible. Public unions know this. Here lies the constitutional flaw of public unions: Elected officials are supposed to govern for the common good, not cede control to unaccountable public employees.

Chapter 3:
How Public Employment
Is Supposed to Work

*"At every stage of the governmental hierarchy
considerable discretion must be granted …"*

—Friedrich Hayek

Putting the union genie back in the bottle also requires a
vision of what replaces it. President Trump had an idea of
how to deal with unmanageable civil servants—basically
to make all senior civil servants terminable at will if they
didn't do what he said. Trump's executive order—creating a civil service "Schedule F"—raised fears of a new
spoils system and was revoked by President Biden. But
alternative public service models aren't limited to either
the union stranglehold or a new spoils system.

What's needed is a modern version of the Progressive
ideal of professional civil service—basically, that public
employees should be hired and evaluated on the basis of
merit and should be held to ethical standards of loyalty to
the public good, not self-interest or partisanship. These

principles are not controversial. But any new framework must embrace the human authority needed to implement a merit system. There's no automatic system that can make these personnel decisions. Human judgment is required, not objective proof in a legal proceeding. How do you prove who doesn't pull his weight, or bores students, or undermines morale by selfish behavior?

There's a tendency to see a government as a giant machine, but the Constitution creates a framework for human responsibility. Leaving aside formulaic services such as Social Security, most of what government does depends on human skill and will. Human agency, not thick rule books and lengthy legal proceedings, is the activating constitutional mechanism for American government.

During the debates over ratifying the Constitution, the antifederalists opposed the Constitution because of the absence of explicit restrictions on official power. But Madison, Hamilton, and Jay argued that the Constitution protects against abuses of power by separating powers so that each branch could check the others. Madison emphasized that "each department should have a will of its own." The greatest danger, Madison believed, was for power to be consolidated into any "self-appointed authority" because "a power independent of the society ... may possibly be turned against both parties."

Accountability all around is the protective system of the Constitution. The branches hold each other accountable. The ballot box is how voters hold elected officials accountable. Accountability down the line is how elected leaders manage the public employees performing the work. The functioning of democracy thus depends, James Madison noted, on an unbroken "chain of dependence … the lowest officers, the middle grade, and the highest, will depend, as they ought, on the President."

But there is inexorable drive, as Madison feared, by government insiders to entrench themselves. Economist Mark Zupan details in *Inside Job* how pharaohs, Mughals, beys, and European kings all found themselves pushed around by a permanent class of inside bureaucrats. The framers hoped that democratic elections would provide the mechanism for guarding against ossification—new leaders would be able to dislodge recalcitrant officials.

The new American republic proved not immune, however, from historical trends toward insider entrenchment. After their defeat in the election of 1800, the Federalists rushed to hand out public jobs to loyalists, including over fifty lifetime judicial appointments. Federal jobs had little turnover and, by the 1820s, had become sinecures rife with inefficiency and corruption.

Andrew Jackson in 1829 ended the tenure of the professional Federalists by instituting a policy of "rotation in office." Appointing officials based on political loyalty was intended as a good government reform, making government more responsive by aligning public jobs with the political majority. But Jackson's system of rotation soon degenerated into the spoils system, resulting in the twin evils of incompetent public employees and disruptive turnover with each change of party control.

Numerous efforts to replace the spoils system with a nonpartisan civil service system got nowhere until the assassination of President Garfield in 1881 by a disappointed job seeker. Contrary to broad misconceptions, civil service did not provide for tenure. The idea was that public employees would get and keep their jobs based on merit—that's why it was called the merit system. The Pendleton Act of 1883 creating civil service "did not restrict the President's general power to remove employees." This was understood both as a constitutional imperative and also as a clear policy guideline that any merit system must include accountability based on performance.

The ideal of meritorious public service, continuing to today, means impartial execution for the common good. "Administration," Woodrow Wilson wrote in 1887, "lies outside the proper sphere of politics." Instead of party hacks, the public would be served by officials with "skill, ability, fidelity, zeal and integrity." Political leaders set priorities and allocate budgets, and public employees have the duty to accomplish public goals to the best of their ability. Political neutrality of public employees had also been the vision of the framers. Thomas Jefferson issued an order barring federal employees from "tak[ing] any part in the business of electioneering, that being inconsistent with the spirit of the Constitution and his duties to it."

A historical halo hovers over civil service because it replaced the spoils system in which public jobs were handed out to political hacks. But civil service was a mainly a *hiring* reform—not a form of job protection. As reform leader George William Curtis said, "if the front door [is] properly tended, the back door [will] take care of itself":

> Having annulled all reason for the improper exercise of the power of dismissal [i.e., jobs were no longer distributed as spoils], we hold that it is better to take the risk of occasional injustice from passion and prejudice, which no law or regulation can control, than to seal up incompetency, negligence, insubordination, insolence, and every other mischief in the service, by requiring a virtual trial at law before an unfit or incapable clerk can be removed.

The new civil service system was also not immune, however, to the historical pattern of insider entrenchment. Initially civil service only encompassed 10 percent of federal workers, but successive presidents expanded it by "blanketing" political supporters into permanent jobs. The growing power of civil servants induced President McKinley to issue an executive order, ostensibly to prevent politically motivated firings, requiring "no removal ... except for just cause and upon written charges."

Tenure conflicted with the original goal of a merit system, however, and the Civil Service Commission was concerned that this order "would give a permanency of tenure in the public service quite inconsistent with the efficiency of the service." In 1902, President Theodore Roosevelt clarified the order: "Nothing contained in said rule shall be construed to require the examination of witnesses or any trial or hearing." These executive orders were codified in the Lloyd-LaFollette Act of 1912— requiring notice in writing, a chance to respond in writing, but no "examination of witnesses, trial, or hearing." The upshot of these changes, in the words of civil service scholar Gerald Frug, was "merely that the executive had to have a legitimate, non-political reason for removal."

The potential for public service was on full display in the New Deal. In 1933, within two months of being named head of the Civilian Works Administration, Harry Hopkins had hired 2.6 million unemployed Americans. The operating philosophy of the FDR administration was to empower people to get the job done. As the 1937 Brownlow Committee put it, "Government is a human institution ... It is certainly not a machine ... What we want is not the streamlined, chromium-trimmed government that looks well in the advertisement, but one that will actually deliver the goods in practice."

The ideal of a merit system focused on achieving public goals remains the vision for advocates of good government. But proposed reforms by Paul Volcker and others have gotten nowhere, for one principal reason: public unions oppose any reform aimed at reintroducing merit or other forms of accountability.

SECTION II:
Public Employee Unions Against the Common Good: A Five-Point Indictment

"A government ill executed, whatever it may be in theory, must be, in practice, a bad government."

—Alexander Hamilton, Federalist 70

There's a "constitutional need," as Justice Stephen Breyer put it, "effectively to implement the public's democratically determined will." Government must aspire to be responsive to public needs, and to deliver services fairly and efficiently. Fulfilling this responsibility requires officials to deploy resources, make trade-offs, evaluate personnel, and adapt to circumstances. Whether officials are doing a good job will be manifested in general results and public satisfaction, if not quarterly metrics, and will be subject to periodic judgments by voters.

But most of the choices needed for effective governance have been disabled by union controls. Instead, unions have imposed restrictions and protocols that presume that there is "one correct way" to deliver public services and that any deviation requires union approval.

Union disempowerment of daily management choices is not a legitimate public structure but a repudiation of the constitutional and moral imperatives of democratic governance. Although the extent of the interference varies somewhat by jurisdiction, public employee unions have disabled democratic governance in five principal ways. Public employee unions have:

1) Severed the links of accountability;

2) Rendered government substantially unmanageable with detailed rules and veto powers;

3) Made government unaffordable with opaque benefit packages and compensation manipulations;

4) Changed public policies to the harm of the public good; and,

5) Entrenched these abuses, and made reform practically impossible, through organized political power.

I now address each of these harms to democratic governance.

Chapter 4:
No Accountability

"People we rated 'outstanding' …
are not very functional."

—James B. King, director of the Office of Personnel
Management, in testimony before Congress

"Any government," Paul Volcker observed, "is only as good as its workers." Good teachers can transform thousands of lives. Bad teachers have a converse effect. Economist Eric Hanushek concluded that terminating the bottom 5 to 8 percent of teachers would propel United States students nearly to the top of international science and math ratings. The quality of public employees, including the senior officials who run departments, makes a huge difference to the functioning of our society.

Public unions have broken the chain of democratic accountability. Police chiefs, school principals, and government supervisors at all levels have lost their ability to make the judgments about who's doing the job and who's not.

In 2017, Reuters compiled a report on police officers with records of repeatedly abusing innocent people. One officer brutally beat up a college student who was sitting on a bench with friends for the alleged crime of drinking a beer in public. That officer had been the subject of forty complaints of misconduct and similar abuses. But most bad officers, Reuters found, could not be dismissed. Why? The rule in public union contracts requires that prior complaints and infractions be expunged from the record, in some jurisdictions after a few months, so it's almost impossible for supervisors to terminate repeat offenders.

A 2017 *Washington Post* report on police discipline examined data from thirty-seven large cities and found a dismissal rate of less than two-tenths of 1 percent, or 130 officers per year out of 91,000. The process is so stacked that police chiefs don't even try for dismissal except in the most outrageous cases, and even then termination or discipline is often overturned by arbitrators. Between 2006 and 2017, over 70 percent of San Antonio police officers fired for cause were rehired on appeal to arbitration.

While there's no centralized database that tracks public employee dismissals and other discipline, the reports from the different public sectors confirm that accountability for performance is negligible—only a small fraction of 1 percent for nonprovisional public employees. About 0.2 percent of Connecticut public employees were fired for work performance issues between February 2018 and February 2019, fewer than 140 in a workforce of over 30,000. In the private sector, by contrast, both terminations and overall turnover are multiples higher.

Terry Moe compiled teacher termination data in his 2011 book, *Special Interest*. In New York City, "eight teachers out of a total teaching force of 55,000 were dismissed for poor performance in 2006–07: a dismissal rate of about one one-hundredth of 1 percent." Illinois was even worse, with only two teachers out of 95,000 dismissed for poor performance annually over an eighteen-year study period. "Dismissing a tenured teacher is not a process," as one superintendent put it. "It's a career."

The poison pill that kills accountability is the replacement of supervisors' judgments with the requirement of objective proof. Who is the supervisor to judge? The supervisor's burden of proof not only requires justifying perceptions of an employee's performance but to establish perfect compliance with detailed procedures. Any foot fault or managerial omission is grounds to bar accountability. Thus, in one hearing observed by journalist Steven Brill, where a shockingly neglectful teacher had not even bothered to grade papers, the teacher's defense was that the school presented no evidence that part of the teacher's job was to grade papers.

For police, the procedural trip wires typically include: inability to interview the officer about what happened without advance notice; allowing the officer to see other people's testimony first so he can try to align his story; appeal to arbitrators who have been individually approved by the police union; no disclosure of past misconduct to

arbitrators unless it occurred recently; several further levels of appeal, again to approved panels of arbitrators; a
requirement to keep all evidence and proceedings private,
so that the public has no transparency to how the police
department is run; and continuing to receive full pay until all appeals are exhausted. With procedures like these,
how could the Minneapolis police chief possibly succeed
in proving that Derek Chauvin was too "tightly wound"
to be on the beat?

For federal civil servants, statutory procedures include a formal process where the supervisor creates a
formal "performance improvement plan," gives the employee a chance to remedy the problems, then another
evaluation, and several levels of appeals. The National
Treasury Employees Union collective bargaining agreement provides eleven factors the supervisor must consider
before taking any disciplinary action. That's eleven arguments for the union lawyer to make in the required legal
hearings. Did the supervisor consider "the consistency of
the penalty with those imposed upon other employees
for the same or similar offenses"; "the clarity with which
the employee was on notice of any rules that were violated"; the "potential for the employee's rehabilitation"; any
"mitigating circumstances… such as unusual job tensions,
personality problems"; and so forth.

The party line by unions is that they don't defend
poor performers. But everyone knows that's not true.
Zero accountability is what unions strive for: "I'm here
to defend even the worst people," said one union official.

A union lawyer stated bluntly: "If I'm representing them, it's impossible to get them out. It's impossible. Unless they commit a lewd act."

Accountability is commonly misunderstood as mainly involving the rights of an employee. Unions put every personnel decision under a legal microscope and argue about it for years. But how about the rights of students to be protected against lousy teachers, and the harm to the public of abusive cops? How about the rights of all the good cops and good teachers who are discouraged by having to work with people who, for whatever reason, can't perform?

Even a small percentage of inadequate teachers, Moe concludes, is hugely destructive: "If we assume that only 5 percent of the nation's public school teachers are not sufficiently competent to be in the classroom—which is probably a very conservative estimate in light of the … data—this means that more than 2.5 million American kids are stuck in classrooms with teachers who are incapable of teaching them."

But the cost of no accountability is far larger than the sum of bad teachers and inept bureaucrats. Accountability protects the integrity of the group within which each of us achieves our goals. Good schools, trustworthy police, efficient government, a successful business, a happy family, and democracy itself … they all are sustained on the expectation that others will do their part or else be accountable. Accountability is primarily a matter of fairness for the group, not the individual.

The harm of no accountability is not legions of bad public employees, but a sluggish, hard-to-manage public culture. The many good people in government find themselves mired in a school or department without the camaraderie of mutual commitment. Doing what's right is supplanted by a sense of futility and fatalism.

No accountability also breeds resistance to change. Supervisors lack the authority to get public employees to do things differently. When there's no sanction, public employees feel free to ignore the direction of new leaders. There's an acronym for it—"WEBEHWYG" (pronounced We-be-wig): "We'll be here when you're gone." Fear of accountability, by contrast, is a powerful driver of hard choices—for example, breaking through the "code of silence" among police officers. Fear of accountability is also a disincentive for abuses of power.

How should accountability decisions be made? Give people responsibility and then let supervisory officials make judgments about performance. That's their job. Abandon the legal requirement that supervisors prove performance traits that are not susceptible to objective proof, such as competence, energy, and effectiveness. It is not hard to protect against arbitrary or unfair decisions: Just give a workers' committee the authority to weigh in or veto the decision. But those reviews must also be based on the perceptions of coworkers, not legal sophistry. Fair accountability is impossible without the exercise of human judgment.

The paradox of accountability is that once it's available, it rarely needs to be exercised. What's important, as noted earlier, is the *availability of accountability*. Once mutual trust and obligation are established, an energetic and cooperative culture leads people to do their best. The prospect of accountability ensures that everyone rows hard, and in the same direction. Accountability also liberates everyone from mind-numbing bureaucracy; there's no need to dictate exactly how to get things done if people can be accountable when they don't.

Democracy without accountability is a machine operating on low voltage, with all the parts and resources, but without the electricity required to make things work. By blocking the authority to hold public employees accountable, public unions drained much of the human energy from democracy.

Chapter 5:
Unmanageable Government

"I need some of my management rights back."

—James Tilton,
California Department of Corrections

Politicians and pundits argue about public policy, but how government works day to day is far more important to most citizens. The controls exercised by public unions—in multi-hundred-page bargaining agreements and in second-guessing by on-site union reps—make responsive, efficient governing a herculean task. The simplest choices must be negotiated as a matter of union entitlements.

Union bargaining agreements presume that governing is like a software program, where following lots of rules produces good results. But governing can't work automatically. Most public jobs—for example, police and teachers—require perception on the spot and judgment. The traits of effective teachers, studies find, are highly idiosyncratic and astonishingly complex. Policing requires instincts, restraint, and street-level psychology, with the overlay of real danger. Even jobs that sound simple require human judgment on the spot—digging a hole for a pole—management expert Chester Barnard observed, involves a few deliberate choices and then many more that no one planned for … avoiding the trees, being alert not to dig into gas lines, and so forth.

The human element of accomplishment is even more complex and idiosyncratic in joint activities. Governing not only requires supervisory judgments about personnel, but it also requires coordinating people, allocating resources effectively, and continually adapting to new needs and circumstances. This is the job of public managers.

What good organizations have in common is a culture of people at all levels taking responsibility.

Responsibility embodies a goal and the authority to use your judgment to get there. Human responsibility is the activating force of America's constitutional government. As James Madison put it,

> It is one of the most prominent features of the Constitution, a principle that pervades the whole system, that there should be the highest possible degree of responsibility in all the Executive officers thereof; any thing, therefore, which tends to lessen this responsibility is contrary to its spirit and intention …

Thomas Edison expressed the same idea more directly: "Nothing that's any good works by itself … You got to make the damn thing work."

James Madison could hardly have imagined what's happened to American government. Basic management choices are precluded or skewed by thick collective bargaining agreements, plus dense civil service rule books and statutory work codes. "If the contract were all about wages and benefits," DiSalvo observes, "contracts would be about 10 pages long." Instead, public choices are hamstrung by rules that function as if designed to make government work badly.

Supervisory restrictions vary by job and by jurisdiction, but the common thread is unmanageability. In most of 2021 and 2022, over one thousand correctional officers at New York City's Rikers Island jail were out on sick days or were unavailable to oversee inmates. That's because their collective bargaining agreement allows unlimited sick days and also gives officers with seniority the right to have no contact with inmates. The result was that "no one was manning dozens of posts at the jail. Cell doors are broken … Inmates in some housing units have been able to come and go as they please."

Unions not only impose rules but also view their role as negotiating any supervisory decision that is in any way discretionary. "Virtually any idea for saving money through outsourcing or consolidation of services," as E. J. McMahon and Terry O'Neil describe in their essay "Taylor Made," "must first be negotiated and agreed to by the union representing the employees who currently provide the service." "'Mere monetary savings,'" under rulings from New York's Public Employment Relations

Board, are "'insufficient' to overcome an employer's obligation to fully bargain the topic."

Here is a short summary of the spider's webs of union mandates that entangle public supervisors:

Schools: In many states, schools are more or less unmanageable. Work rules have removed principals' authority to decide which teachers are best, or who should be given a different responsibility, or who should be laid off when there's a budget cut. Those decisions must be made strictly on the basis of seniority. This ensures, Terry Moe found, "that excellent teachers will be automatically fired if they happen to have little seniority and that lousy teachers will be automatically retained if they happen to have lots of seniority." For example, in 2012, the Sacramento teacher of the year, sixth-grade teacher Michelle Apperson, had to be laid off because she lacked seniority to survive budget cuts. Compensation is also out of the principal's control. Pay is based on seniority and the number of degrees or certificates a teacher gets—even though studies show that teacher quality is not correlated with either seniority or degrees.

The granularity of work rules makes even the most rudimentary supervisory tasks difficult. The New York City teachers union contract is "an extraordinary document," former schools chancellor Joel Klein observed, "running for hundreds of pages, governing who can teach what and when, who can be assigned to hall-monitor or lunchroom duty and who can't, who has to be given time off to do union work during the school day, and so on." Terry Moe reflected that "It's too bad all Americans can't just sit down and read the collective bargaining contracts their school districts have to live by. Many people, I hazard to guess, would be stunned." Moe lists the following:

—Rules that require principals to give advance notice to teachers before visiting their classrooms to evaluate their performance,

—Rules that prohibit the use of standardized student tests for evaluating teacher performance,

—Rules that specify all the procedures that must be followed—in setting up an "improvement program," monitoring, reporting, mentoring, and so forth—if a teacher is evaluated as unsatisfactory,

—Rules that give teachers guaranteed preparation times of a specified number of minutes a day,

—Rules that limit the number of faculty meetings and their duration,

—Rules that limit the number of parent conferences and other forums in which teachers meet with parents,

—Rules that limit how many minutes teachers can be required to be on campus before and after school,

—Rules that limit class size,

—Rules that limit the nonteaching duties that teachers can be asked to perform, such as yard duty, hall duty, or lunch duty,

—Rules that allow teachers to take paid sabbaticals,

—Rules that allow teachers to accumulate unused sick leave for years and eventually to convert it into cash windfalls,

—Rules that provide for complicated, time-consuming grievance procedures that teachers can invoke if they feel their job rights have somehow been violated,

—Rules that give teachers who are union officials time off to perform union duties (which means their classes must be taught by substitutes).

Any one of these rules might be okay, but cumulatively they add up to personnel policies where there's always a reason not to do what's needed. "Who in their right mind, if they were organizing the schools for the benefit of children," Moe observes, "would organize them in this way?"

But schools are not organized to do what's best for America's youth. One rookie teacher I interviewed recounted his surprise when, at the organizing meeting at the beginning of the school year, half the teachers got up and left in the middle of the presentation: the required forty minutes with the principal were up. Pity the teacher who actually wants to help out. A teacher I interviewed from Boston made the mistake of volunteering to supervise a new breakfast program for poor students and found herself dressed down by the union rep: "There is no breakfast duty. In the last contract, it didn't come up. We didn't negotiate it. There IS NO breakfast duty. I don't care who wants to do it, there is no breakfast duty."

The addiction of entitlements is hard for teachers to resist, however. In many schools, sick days and professional development days are now, as a matter of course, treated as vacation days and usually fall on either side of the weekend. One report in Seattle found that its tenured teacher absences comprised 9 percent of all school days, which meant that 56,000 instructional days in Seattle in one year were taught by substitute teachers. On the days with substitute teachers, educators say, the students generally learn little to nothing.

America's public schools are not only in the vise grip of teachers unions, but other unions as well, including janitorial staff and lunchroom workers. When she was on the New York City Council, Eva Moskowitz held hearings on union contracts and discovered why paint was flaking in schools at the top of walls—the union contract only allowed custodians to paint up to ten feet; any higher and the school would have to pay extra to hire a member of the painters' union to complete the work. In another incident, when asked to clean up a spill in the school cafeteria, the janitor refused, because the contract only required cleaning on Friday.

In her 2015 book, *The Prize*, Dale Russakoff described what happened with Mark Zuckerberg's pledge of $100 million to improve Newark, New Jersey, schools. One of the protagonists in the book is a young teacher, gifted and caring, who is committed to the public school system. After several years, she quits and joins a nearby KIPP charter school. When asked why, she explained that Newark schools could only afford one teacher in a classroom of twenty-three students, and she could not provide the attention each student needed. The charter school, by contrast, had two teachers in each classroom and access to a learning specialist.

How could the charter school afford three teachers per class? It wasn't a matter of more funding: the charter school spent *$3,000 less per student* than the Newark public school. Newark couldn't afford more teachers because of inefficiencies and costs embedded in its structures, especially its union contracts. Janitorial services in Newark schools cost $1,200 per student, for example, compared with $400 per student at the charter school. Nor did Zuckerberg's money improve staffing; most of it went in retroactive payments to teachers, as the union required in the collective bargaining agreement.

The harm done to generations of American students is not an accident but is the deliberate exercise of union political power, now enshrined in layers of law. "The more restrictive the contract," studies show, "the lower the gains in student achievement."

There are many good schools, but their common thread is that they have cultures in which educators basically ignore the rules. It would be a challenge to find any good school where teachers focus on their entitlements.

Inefficiency as Union Prerogative

The labyrinth of union rules and entitlements in schools is mirrored in varying degrees in most areas of public service. It's an odd phenomenon, in which unions promote a work culture aimed at doing what's wrong. Like a warped personal relationship, public unions seem preoccupied with showing who's really in charge, not doing what's best for society.

Managing is often treated as an affront, intruding on employee prerogatives. When former Indianapolis mayor Stephen Goldsmith joined the Bloomberg administration as New York City's deputy mayor, he tried to walk through different departments to get public employees' ideas on how better to do things. But he was told that would violate the union prohibition on "direct dealing"; any discussion of managerial ideas had to be negotiated with union officials.

Inefficiency is often mandated by contract. Garbage collection in New York, for example, costs $431 per ton, or twice as much as private carters in New York, because of rigid work rules on routes, hours of pickup, mandated bonuses unrelated to performance, and other contractual inefficiencies. In Chicago in 2011, Daniel DiSalvo reports, "the garbage truck routes, worked out through union contracts and ward politics, are an amazing maze that wears down the trucks and wastes fuel and employees' time. Trash disposal in the Windy City costs $231 per ton compared to $129 in Los Angeles and $74 in Dallas."

Other rules exist just to milk the system. At one point, engineers on the Long Island Railroad got an extra day's pay if they cleaned the train windshield. A series of articles on LIRR work practices found that engineers got double pay if they operated a diesel and an electric engine in the same shift; gave maintenance workers the option of not working on rainy days but paying them for two hours nonetheless; paid engineers for eight hours if they moved a locomotive in a maintenance yard (a one-hour task); and required any new maintenance assignment to last at least three weeks. As with teacher sick days, gaming the system is considered an entitlement, not an abuse of public trust.

A short culvert on the road where I live took eighteen months to fix, with giant yellow machinery unused on the side of the road for weeks on end. As I watched nothing happen, I began to suspect that American government at this point has a culture of unmanageability. Put yourself in the shoes of a supervisor. When almost any task requires negotiating a thicket of worker restrictions, why bother? That things get done at all is a testament to countless public employees who make things work even when, like Gulliver in Lilliput, they are tied down by countless rules.

Unions and the Public Good: Just Say No

Officials are regularly confronted with challenges and crises that no one predicted. In these situations, officials need to adapt and to redeploy resources. But public unions see their responsibilities as bounded by the literal terms of their contracts. Any deviation in routine, no matter how insignificant or how large, provides a basis to refuse to pitch in. The COVID pandemic exposed the true colors of the teachers unions. While nurses, grocery store clerks, deliverymen, and other essential workers went to work so the rest of society could function, teachers refused to come back for almost two years.

American Federation of Teachers president Randi Weingarten in 2020 said that the union planned to stop school reopenings "until we get the virus under control." "Nothing is off the table," Weingarten threatened—"not advocacy or protests, negotiations, grievances, or lawsuits" or even "safety strikes." Indeed, most public schools remained closed during the 2020–2021 school year, while most parochial and private schools reopened.

The unions also resisted distance learning, arguing that it wasn't specified in their contracts. American Enterprise Institute scholar Frederick M. Hess followed the trail of union resistance with disbelief:

> [The Los Angeles union imposed] heavy restrictions around virtual learning—including provisions stating that teachers could not be required to provide live remote instruction or *even to work during the school day.* In Brevard County, Florida, the union and district agreed to a memorandum of agreement (MOU) that capped teachers' instructional time at three hours per day. In Boston, the union-district MOU imposed a two-hour limit on synchronous (live) instruction.

As the COVID closure continued, studies confirmed that the harm to students and families was substantial, especially the poor and minorities. As *New York* magazine columnist Jonathan Chait reports, "Many of the poorest students with the least stable home lives—one analysis estimates the figure at around 3 million—never logged on or performed any schoolwork at all over the last year." One education assessment group found that Black third graders performed 17 percentile points lower than the same cohort had two years before. White third graders were lower by 9 percentile points. Other studies chronicled an epidemic of mental health issues caused by the isolation of teenagers.

As the evidence mounted of cascading harms from closed schools—dramatic learning loss that will take years to recover, parents without child care unable to go to work, emotional harm to students of all ages—the teachers union advocates argued that "learning loss" was not significant and certainly not outweighed by the risk to teachers.

While COVID was considered too dangerous to reopen schools, it was not so dangerous that teachers could be required to be vaccinated. Union leader Randi Weingarten: "Vaccinations must be negotiated between employers and workers, not coerced."

There was nothing any elected leader could do about it except try to come up with inducements. Collective bargaining agreements had preempted the authority of public officials to manage schools during this crisis.

Chapter 6:
Unaffordable Benefits, Hidden from Taxpayers and Paid by Our Children

"The ultimate question for a responsible man to ask is ... how the coming generation is to live."

—Dietrich Bonhoeffer

Every public dollar involves a moral choice. A dollar wasted is a dollar not available for some other worthy goal. Every neglected public need—whether to help the hungry, deal with climate change, fix the roads, or reduce tax burdens—has been compromised by the budgetary grip of public employee unions. Public unions' indifference to wasteful inefficiency is matched by their rapacity in demanding benefits in the future that are not reasonably affordable.

Good public employees deserve fair compensation as well as respect for their public service. Many public employees in America, particularly those with important responsibility, are underpaid. Judges, for example, are paid about the same as junior associates at a big-city law firm. Teacher pay in some states is not much better than that for unskilled manual labor. An overhaul of public employment should be accompanied by a reset of compensation levels aimed at attracting good candidates.

Public pay should be transparent to taxpayers, however, and not prone to abuse. Instead, public unions have negotiated contracts that encourage manipulation and fiscally irresponsible practices. Elected officials have been complicit—to attract union political support today, politicians agreed to long-term pension and health benefits without a plan to fund them. Instead of paying into the system as obligations were incurred, many states, under pressure from public unions, kicked the can down the road so as not to cut current services. As the deficit reached scandalous proportions in recent years, states started moderating the benefits for new hires but did little to relieve many states and municipalities from the fiscal vise.

Unfunded benefit liabilities made up 40 percent of the $18 billion in debt that forced the city of Detroit to declare bankruptcy in 2013. In 2012, Mayor Michael Bloomberg claimed that "every penny" of personal income tax collected by New York City went straight to pension payments. A 2021 Moody's report found that Illinois's state pension liability (not even including municipal pensions) was so high that every household in the state would need to pay $65,000 to cover the difference.

How to cure these deficits is unclear. The states with the largest deficits are already losing population because of high taxes and aging demographics. A study by the Urban Institute found that new state employees in New

Jersey had to pay more into the pension plan than they would ever get back—unwittingly subsidizing older retirees. Some observers have suggested that bankruptcy, not currently allowed for states, is the only realistic solution for Illinois and certain other states.

The pressure to cut current services is enormous. Des Moines cut library hours and reduced street cleaning to make up for pension-driven budget shortfalls. Rockford, Illinois, may soon sell its municipal water system. Pasadena cut over 120 local jobs, including numerous police positions, and reduced transit service after facing insurmountable pension liabilities. Oakland in 2010 laid off eighty police officers, during a crime wave, in order to fund retirement obligations.

Clawing our way out of these public deficits requires doing everything possible to deliver government more efficiently. Instead, public unions not only shackle public executives with inefficient work rules, as discussed above, but have designed a public compensation system that is unsustainable. The bottom line is that taxpayers are on the hook for pension and health-care obligations far greater than in the private sector.

The fact that these benefits are largely hidden from public view does not reflect well on the motives of unions and their political enablers. As political scientists Sarah Anzia and Terry Moe explain, "Health and pension benefits are extremely complicated, difficult for the public to understand, difficult for the media to convey—and thus nearly invisible politically." Public employee unions have focused their demands on this "electoral blind spot," with the cooperation of elected officials who will be out of office when the bill comes due. Unions then protect themselves against the inevitable fiscal downfall by getting statutory and constitutional protection against future impairment. The playbook, as described by economist Jeffrey Dorman, resembles a criminal scheme, not business as usual:

> The basic process by which states get in such severe financial trouble is well-established. Unions get protection from any future diminishing of pension obligations enshrined into state law or, ideally, the state constitution. Then public sector unions give state politicians big campaign contributions in exchange for large, fiscally irresponsible future pension benefits. The state legislature then underfunds those pensions, keeping the taxpayers from realizing the full cost of the promised pensions and eliminating the near term pain from the pension promises. Unions don't object to the underfunding because they know the law protects their pensions no matter how bad the situation gets. Eventually, you are Illinois, with a pension shortfall equal to roughly eighteen months of total state spending.

Fair compensation is in the eye of the beholder and, in a functioning democracy, should be an issue that candidates debate. But that hasn't happened, because transparency would reveal what taxpayers must pay. This is part of the formula for enriching insiders that economist Mark Zupan calls "slack." The more slack, the more public unions can skim without public outrage.

The accounting rules for public obligations have now changed, so that long-term obligations can no longer be completely hidden from the public. But the horse has left the barn, and there's still little transparency on how the obligations pile up. How is it that 40,000 public employees in California receive over $100,000 in pensions? That's at least $4 billion every year. In Illinois, 20,000 retirees get over $100,000. In many cities and states, inflating pensions continues to be a common practice.

The following games and manipulations have inflated benefits for many retirees far beyond what is considered fair and reasonable in the private sector:

Early retirement and double-dipping. Most employees in America work until at least age sixty-five and build up their retirement accounts in upward of forty or more years of work. Under collective bargaining agreements, many public employees are entitled to "retire" with full pensions after twenty-five or thirty years of service, often in their forties and fifties. California allows many state workers to retire at fifty-five with pensions that exceed their actual salaries. Police, firefighters, and other public safety employees are often accorded benefits more like military personnel, and they have long been entitled to "retire" after twenty years with pensions that, in cities like Orlando, are 70 percent of their highest salary (with annual cost-of-living increases).

The city may be on the hook for retirement payouts for forty-plus years.

Allowing public employees to retire far in advance of actual retirement means that the number receiving retirement benefits on the public purse is about 25 percent greater than would be the case in the private sector. Within the next fifteen years, CalPERS, California's state retirement pension system, will have twice as many pensioners as current workers. Retiring with full benefits ten years early, as an actuarial matter, can double the cost of benefits.

Early retirement is a good deal for public employees, if not for taxpayers, also because many of these so-called retirees immediately "double-dip" by coming back to work in government. *Eighty percent* of New Jersey sheriffs double-dipped in 2012. Almost 10 percent of Oregon's public employees double-dipped in 2019, including a provost at the University of Oregon who received $148,000 in pension payments on top of her $160,000 salary. Sometimes these additional public sector stints entitle employees to separate pension benefits, as in the case of the village official in Illinois who pulled down three separate pensions by the time of his "final" retirement.

Spiking pensions with extra overtime and disability claims. "Spiking" is the practice of increasing salaries in the final years of employment to inflate an employee's retirement pay. Claiming disability near retirement is so rampant among police departments that the practice is referred to as "Chief's Disease." A 2020 report on Illinois teachers found that between 40 and 50 percent of teachers had experienced "unexpectedly large increases in their compensation during the years used as the base for their pensions."

Spiking can take several forms, but the two most common are:

—A glut of overtime work or banked vacation time in the final years of employment. Perhaps the most extreme case was by Long Island Railroad chief measurement operator Thomas Caputo, who in 2018 logged 3,864 hours of overtime, the equivalent of 483 eight-hour days in addition to his regular job. The extra hours boosted his pay over $300,000 above his base salary. After a newspaper exposé, he was caught and convicted of fraud. Otherwise, all the overtime he claimed would have boosted his final pension by over $93,000 a year. In 2008, a fire chief in Contra Costa County, California, "sold back" over five hundred hours of vacation time, raising his pension by nearly 50 percent, for an additional $6,000 per month.

—A sudden promotion or reassignment just before retirement. For example, a police lieutenant who was suddenly promoted to the rank of battalion chief for his final year, raising his pension by $25,000 per year.

The 2020 Illinois report found that spiking alone had added potentially hundreds of millions of dollars of additional liabilities to the balance sheets of the state's teacher retirement systems.

In recent years several states have tried to limit the worst abuses of spiking and similar scams, but the retiree ranks in those states are collecting inflated pensions that taxpayers and their children must pay for decades.

Rich health plans. In the private sector, workers typically contribute a significant portion of their current health-care costs—about 20 percent for individual plans on average—and often can economize by choosing a lower-cost plan among several offered. When they retire, they are entitled to Medicare.

In government, by contrast, unions have successfully bargained or lobbied for lifetime health-care coverage for current and retired employees that requires only minimal employee contributions. According to the National Conference of State Legislatures, states on average cover 92 percent of employee health-care costs.

In New York City, many public employees contribute zero to their health-care costs, and most receive free coverage after retirement. If NYC employees contributed only 10 percent of health-care costs, New York City would have an additional $800 million annually to spend on essential public services. Instead, the municipal unions fiercely resist even modest ways to economize on health care. New York City in 2021 proposed to move retirees to Medicare Advantage, a public option that bundles more health-care services than Medicare into a privately administered plan; it was projected to save the city $600 million a year. The unions staged demonstrations and then succeeded in getting a court ruling that their health benefits could not be changed.

Making our children pay. Most public pensions are defined benefit plans, in which the retiree is promised an annuity in a fixed amount, plus negotiated cost-of-living increases. By contrast, over 75 percent of private retiree accounts are defined contribution plans, in which the size of the ultimate nest egg is dependent on investment returns on the retiree's 401(k) or other retirement account.

Defined benefit plans, with early retirement, are much richer than contribution plans for long-term employees. In a 2013 paper, Professor Thom Reilly showed that public sector employees could expect to collect almost twice as much in postretirement benefits as their private sector counterparts, and over 50 percent more in lifetime average compensation when retirement benefits are factored in. A 2012 study similarly found that "employees of all levels of government generally have substantially more pension wealth than their private sector counterparts."

Theoretically the state or municipality could set aside enough taxpayer revenue each year to keep pace with its actuarial obligations. But for decades, public employee unions actively prevented governors from coming to terms with the growing shortfall in pension funds. Teachers and cops would have to be laid off. Taxpayers would then see what unaffordable retiree promises had wrought.

In New Jersey, for example, public unions beat back pension reforms for decades. In 1984 Governor Tom Kean created a Pension Study Commission to recommend how to bring state finances back in line. The commission recommended increasing the retirement age and creating a less expensive system for new employees. Teachers union president Edithe Fulton attacked the report as an "outrageous assault ... on the state pension system" and called for a boycott of businesses of citizens who served on the commission. The recommendations were never implemented. In 1991, Governor Jim Florio decentralized pension responsibility to local school districts, which might take future obligations more seriously. Wielding awesome political power that I will shortly discuss, the teachers union orchestrated a political coup to reverse the decision. In 2006, Governor Jon Corzine called a special legislative session to deal with rising pension and benefit costs. Public unions also blocked most of the proposed legislative reforms.

By 2012, when government accounting rules were finally aligned with the better practices in the private sector, the retiree deficit hole in New Jersey was too deep to see any way out. An independent commission concluded in 2015 that fully funding its benefit liabilities was "no longer within the State's means ... not only because of the dollar amount of funding required, but also because a State budget so burdened by employee benefits would not be able to weather a recession or permit the State to do what is necessary to promote the general welfare of its citizens." Five years after the report was published, the reserves needed to pay these obligations had declined further.

Most of the huge debt for public employee benefits in the future, incurred largely as a result of union demands, will not come due during the tenure of the political leaders who acceded to it, nor indeed to the voters at that time. Our children must pay the bill.

Chapter 7:
Public Policy Against
the Public Interest

*"We have produced politics by a hidden elite,
unaccountable, unresponsive, and often
unconcerned with any larger public interest."*

—Fareed Zakaria

The duty of public servants is to serve the public, not themselves. Instead, public unions have mobilized political power to change the goals of government to benefit public employees, almost always to the public's harm. In 2021, the Citizens Budget Commission in New York reported twenty-one new union-sponsored bills in the state legislature aimed at increasing public employee pensions and benefits—in a state already reeling from the budgetary weight of pensioners.

The steady diet of union-sponsored policy initiatives and reform blockers has materially altered the functioning of criminal justice, schools, social services, and other vital government functions.

Changing Criminal Justice

In 1994, the California Correctional Peace Officers Association (CCPOA) organized a coalition to pass a referendum for a "three-strikes" law mandating twenty-five years–to–life sentences for people on their third crime, even if nonviolent. By increasing the number of inmates, the law thereby expanded the need for more correctional officers. One person was sentenced to life imprisonment for attempting to shoplift videotapes from Kmarts.

The union-sponsored law had the desired effect—the California state prison population rose from roughly 50,000 in 1985 to over 170,000 in 2006. So did the number of CCPOA members, from 5,000 to 31,000. So did the compensation of prison guards—to a pay scale roughly twice that in other states.

In Baltimore, in the face of horrific scandals involving effective control of the jails by gang leaders, the correctional officers' union in 2010 was nonetheless able to secure passage of a Correctional Officers Bill of Rights, which made it practically impossible to discipline the officers. The law sailed through the Maryland legislature, *Washington Post* columnist Charles Lane found, because the corrections officers comprise about a quarter of the Maryland membership of AFSCME.

Maryland had also been the first state to enact the Law Enforcement Officers Bill of Rights, which imposes a number of procedural hurdles to any disciplinary action against a police officer—for example, requiring a five-day delay before an officer can be interviewed, and a requirement that the interview be conducted by fellow officers, not an outside investigator. Because of the law, a Baltimore police officer caught in 2017 framing people with fabricated evidence stayed on the payroll for several years. Public outrage caused Maryland to repeal the law in 2021, but fifteen other states have similar laws.

Police unions enjoy a political influence far larger than their actual numbers because their endorsement is courted by Republicans as well as Democrats. Few candidates want to be accused of being "soft on crime."

Even in the face of riots prompted by killings of George Floyd and Breonna Taylor, police unions have been able to defeat or neutralize reformers' calls for civilian oversight boards. About 160 cities have oversight boards (out of 18,000 police departments), but even those are largely toothless. An extensive report by the *Washington Post* in 2021 concluded that civilian oversight boards are "built to fail." After the shooting of Breonna Taylor, for example,

> Louisville's Citizens Commission on Police Accountability could do nothing. As set up, it could initiate no investigations or take complaints from citizens. It could only examine closed internal affairs investigations of police shootings to determine if they were adequate and recommend changes in policy or training. It could not recommend discipline for officers.

In other cities with oversight boards, police unions have sued to remove subpoena rights and other investigative tools, arguing, among other things, that civilian oversight violates the collective bargaining agreement.

Police unions argue that oversight boards are unnecessary and inept. Jim Pasco, executive director of the national Fraternal Order of Police, says civilian oversight boards are "akin to putting a plumber in charge of the investigation of airplane crashes." But reformers point out the oversight boards typically are comprised of lawyers and others with criminal justice backgrounds.

Police oversight is a matter of national importance. The distrust by minority communities is real and often justified. Striking a sensible balance between protecting police and safeguarding against police abuses is vital. The only reason that hasn't happened is that police unions have used their political influence to block it.

Increasing Public Budgets

The failure of America's schools is not, generally, caused by underfunding. America spends more than almost any other country, with worse results. But this was less clear in 1988, when the teachers' union in California promoted a referendum requiring that 40 percent of the total California state general fund be spent on education. That was a full seven percentage points more than California generally spent, and, in today's budget, means that $16 billion is not available to deal with many problems faced by California—including drought, homelessness, and tax flight. Aside from the antidemocratic nature of committing permanently to a fixed percentage of expenditures, where did that 40 percent number come from? It was apparently made up, a nice round number, which unions argued would "ensure stability [and take] school financing out of politics." In fact, most of the increase in school funding went to increasing teachers' salaries, without meaningful improvement in school quality. California's teachers are now among the highest paid in the country, while the performance of California's schools is in the bottom quartile.

Public employee unions usually lead the charge against taxpayer initiatives to limit spending and taxes. In 2009, Daniel DiSalvo reports, "both Washington State and Maine had spending caps on the ballot. In both cases the public sector unions provided between one-third and one-half of the total funding opposing the measures." In 2005 public employee unions led a $28 million effort to defeat a spending cap bill in California. In 1991, the New Jersey teachers unions went to war against Democrats when Governor Jim Florio used part of the budget for tax relief instead of schools.

Public unions can argue that more public spending is good public policy. But, in a democracy, that policy choice should be made by elected officials considering all interests, not just to kowtow to public employees. Public unions instead have built a statutory bulwark against cost saving, even when no conceivable public purpose is served. When first elected governor of New York, Andrew Cuomo faced a budget shortfall and announced he would save $50 million a year by closing an empty juvenile delinquency facility. Then he learned that a New York statute requires at least one year advance notice before closing a facility that has union employees.

Public unions press for long-term budgetary commitments even when, as with retiree benefits, there is no public debate and no reasonable prospect that taxpayers can afford them. The unions also block layoffs and other economizing measures to make up the shortfall. But unions have a plan, as noted, for when the day of reckoning comes: Public unions in Illinois are leading a referendum initiative for a constitutional amendment that would give priority to bargaining agreements over any state law.

Blocking Better Schools

Nowhere does union influence warp vital social policy more than in education. Education policy is largely driven by teachers unions, whose main interest is protecting teachers, not preparing students. They not only demand control, unaccountability, and increased funding, but they also resist initiatives to create alternative schools that many parents want.

The poor performance in inner-city schools, the teachers unions say, is caused by forces beyond their control. Pathetic performance it surely is: Sixth graders in the poorest district are *four grade levels below* students in best school districts. While these differences are not solely caused by ineffective schools, bad schools bear much of the blame. We know this because nonunionized charter schools in the same districts, with students typically chosen by lottery, show dramatically superior results.

Economist Thomas Sowell reviews recent data for New York charter schools that share buildings with public schools. In 70 percent of the classes in KIPP charter schools, a majority of students scored proficient or better in English language arts; the comparable number was 5 percent in the public schools in the same buildings. The math differential was even higher. At Success Academy, a charter school network in Harlem, over three-quarters of students in each of thirty grade levels (the total from several schools) scored at "proficient" or better in English language arts. In a third of the classes, a majority scored "above proficient"—the highest category. In only three of thirty-six grade levels did the adjoining public schools manage a "proficient" rating for majority of students. Not one public school class had a majority of students scoring "above proficient." In 2019, Success Academy 2 in Harlem was ranked thirty-seventh out of all elementary schools in New York State. The public school it shares a building with, PS 30, which serves a third as many kids and spends over twice as much per pupil, was ranked 1,694th.

What is different about Success Academy? Steven Brill concluded that its educators were not shackled to union contracts and prerogatives:

> The Harlem Success teachers' contract drives home the idea that the school is about the children, not the grown-ups. It is one page, allows them to be fired at will, and defines their responsibilities no more specifically than that they

must help the school achieve its mission. Harlem Success teachers are paid about 5 to 10 percent more than union teachers on the other side of the building who have their levels of experience ...

The union contract in place on the public school side of the building is 167 pages. Most of it is about job protection and what teachers can and cannot be asked to do during the 6 hours and 57.5 minutes (8:30 to about 3:25, with 50 minutes off for lunch) of their 179-day work year.

The reaction of teachers unions? Charter schools represent the bull's-eye of union ire. How dare they offer better schools, with open admissions, in the same neighborhoods as failing public schools!

State by state, teachers unions have succeeded in capping the number of charter schools. In Massachusetts in 2016, teachers unions successfully blocked an increase in charter schools after several studies found that "these schools are producing spectacular gains" and that "the effects are particularly large for disadvantaged students." Another union technique is to hurt existing charters in any way possible—such as fighting every decision to let charter schools use extra space in existing school buildings and reducing public funding per student below that of public schools.

Teachers unions also vociferously oppose "parent choice"—for example, providing vouchers that can be used at parochial or private schools. In 1993,

Michael Hartney reports, the California Teachers Association "organized the single largest volunteer phone bank in the history of American state politics. The CTA recruited over 10 percent of the state's entire teacher workforce to make nearly a million calls urging voters to reject Proposition 174, a school-voucher initiative." In California in 2000, the teachers unions spent $21 million to defeat another initiative to allow vouchers. To defeat a proposal for vouchers in Utah in 2007, Terry Moe found, "virtually every penny of the money was contributed by the teachers unions," including "from teachers unions in other states—California, Washington, Colorado, Illinois, New Jersey, Kentucky, Wisconsin, Pennsylvania, and Ohio." Their PAC was named Utahns for Public Schools.

Just as unions don the cloak of "due process" to justify no accountability, they justify opposing charter schools in order to "support public schools." But every once in a while union supporters slip up and admit that the goal is not better schools but protection of teacher jobs. "Education is just one path toward a stronger community," one columnist wrote in the *Washington Post*: "Schools should [also]... enrich communities through employment opportunities." My favorite is this one, found by columnist Jonathan Chait, from a pro-union blog: "We don't need to swap out all the bad and mediocre teachers for better teachers, anymore than we should swap out our struggling students for more advanced students."

Public Policy for Public Unions, not for the Public Good

Public employee union policy initiatives are not episodic but pervasive. Former California State Senate president Gloria Romero (a Democrat) put it this way:

> There is no aspect of state government operations or public policy that is untouched by the power of public-sector unions and their allies in Sacramento … From enacting legislation to writing a state budget to confirming state board and commission appointees, labor's presence is omnipresent. It also includes ghostwriting eleventh-hour legislative changes to push ballot-qualified citizen initiatives to a more obscure ballot position so that their backed initiatives will be seen by voters first. Their influence extends beyond the Legislature, and includes clout with how the state's legal counsel writes ballot summaries and titles.

No political leader is immune from union influence. The flip-flop of President Joe Biden on charter schools is a case in point. The charter school movement got a huge boost by the Race to the Top program initiated by the Obama-Biden administration. As Jonathan Chait recounts,

> In the dozen years since Barack Obama undertook the most dramatic education reform in half a century—prodding local governments to measure how they serve their poorest students and to create alternatives, especially charter

schools ... the evidence for their success has become overwhelming.

But on the campaign trail in 2020, as Chait reports, Joe Biden reversed course: "I am not a charter-school fan because it takes away the options available and money for public schools."

In March 2022, President Biden proposed new regulations that give teachers unions legal knives to kill charters—requiring that charters serve a "diverse population" (instead of the overwhelmingly minority populations), require proof of "unmet demand" because of "over-enrollment of existing public schools" (instead of demand prompted by poor public school quality), and require that the charter collaborate with a "traditional public school" and provide a letter from the public school affirming this partnership—in effect, giving public schools a veto. In a withering column in the *Washington Post*, George Will points to the huge waiting list for charter schools by minority parents and characterizes Biden's position as "tawdry fidelity to a funder."

In the fifty years since public unions consolidated their power through collective bargaining, they have steadily reshaped the policy framework of government. Union influence is unique, compared to all interest groups, and it's not merely one of scale—the union elephant, say, versus all the hyenas. Public employee unions are not just getting some public favors, but they are controlling the public policies on how government operates. Teachers unions prevent public schools from working, and they also prevent any solutions.

No matter which party is elected, no matter what its priorities, the one certainty is that government operations will not be made more efficient, or responsive, or, as with schools and police accountability, even functional. Public employee unions keep it that way by layers of legal armor and by the exercise of brute political force.

Chapter 8:
Not Reformable: The Stranglehold of Public Employee Political Power

"Men wonder to see into how small a number of weak and worthless hands a great people may fall … [and] regulate everything by their own caprice."

—Alexis de Tocqueville

Democrats see public unions as their meal ticket. Republican leaders treat public unions like an unfriendly sovereign power that must be dealt with, even if its demands are unreasonable and cause America harm. Would-be reformers of either party, determined to run government prudently, approach unions hat in hand. Any reforms at the margins come at a high price. With two notable exceptions, every effort to rein in union excesses has resulted in abject political defeat. The unions, meanwhile, continue to tighten their grip over government operations.

What gives public unions this power? Americans supposedly live in a republic in which voters elect leaders to run the operating machinery of government. How is it that public unions hold the keys?

The answer is that, over the past fifty years, public unions have harnessed the power of the state to put themselves in a dominating political position. They have three sources of power, each unique to them:

—Public union political advocacy is in a league of its own, with billions of dollars per year to spend on political influence, plus a pool of millions of members who can be recruited for political activity. State laws authorizing collective bargaining, and allowing automatic deductions of dues, are the catalyst for this mass mobilization of public funds and public workers.

—Public unions have used this political clout over the decades to construct a formidable legal fortress against reform. New leaders come to office with hands tied by collective bargaining agreements and a web of statutory restrictions.

—Public unions hold daily government decisions in their hands and have shown no hesitation to wield every club in their arsenal, including job actions and strikes, to bring political leaders to heel.

The result is a political force unlike any in American history—amassed and entrenched using state power. Like a kind of political jujitsu, unions have weaponized the mass of modern government against democratic reform of modern government. The bigger government gets, the more public employees can be organized against reforming it.

Reformers can't get out of the starting gate. Collective bargaining agreements typically run for three to five years and are not coterminous with election cycles. "A new mayor or governor—no matter how hard-charging a reformer," Daniel DiSalvo concludes, "will often find his or her hands tied by the agreements unions managed to extract from his or her predecessors." A legal presumption against change is now embedded in administrative law, as E. J. McMahon and Terry O'Neil found in New York: Many "outdated, inefficient and expensive 'past practices' [are held] to be binding on public employers." When the Long Island Railroad tried to enforce its contractual right to pay maintenance workers "straight time" for night shifts, arbitrators ruled that the railroad had to pay overtime because of past practices.

Nor can elected leaders achieve meaningful change when collective bargaining agreements come up for renegotiation. The statutes authorizing collective bargaining usually impose upon elected executives a legal duty to negotiate over any matter involving wages, working hours, or other "terms and conditions of employment." If there is an impasse—because, say, an elected executive wants to reduce the union controls—that too is generally beyond the executive's power. In many states, and in the federal government, an impasse over a new agreement is not resolved by elected officials but by arbitrators or other unelected bodies.

In New York State, a law called the Triborough Amendment provides that the existing collective bargaining agreement stays in place until a new agreement is reached—continuing to accrue any automatic "step increases." The union can sit on its hands and lose nothing to a would-be reformer. Rhode Island enacted a similar evergreen collective bargaining law in 2019.

Just as unions can largely ignore elected executives, so too are unions largely immune from their own members. Most states do not require unions to be recertified in periodic elections. In New Jersey, for example, union certification is perpetual unless there's a petition for decertification, which requires signatures of 30 percent of all people in a bargaining group—far more onerous than required to get issues or candidates to the vote in either a democratic or a corporate election. Union members also have a hard time resigning. The National Treasury Employees Union requires resignations to occur only in July and only with the countersignature of a union official who, as one official told me, usually is on vacation during the narrow window for resignations.

Collective bargaining controls are only the first layer of union legal armor. Over the past five decades, unions have steadily used political influence to permanently encase management controls in statutes. Some of the most significant restrictions therefore are not even subject to collective bargaining—including procedures that effectively bar accountability, mandate seniority preferences, impose requirements for a minimum number of sick days, and bar merit pay. Governors, mayors, and other elected executives have no legal authority to override these statutory protections. Daniel DiSalvo reports:

> When then New York governor George Pataki and Albany lawmakers appointed a special authority to handle the distressed finances of Nassau County, Long Island, even that authority couldn't alter union contracts. In a decade under its watch, generous new contracts were negotiated with six-figure salaries for police officers and "strange perks" such as "paid time off for giving blood."

Legislative bodies theoretically can amend or repeal statutes that constrain executive authority. But American democracy is organized to make it difficult to repeal old laws. Often, a few members of a legislative body can exercise their prerogatives to block or delay votes. That's why repealing any interest group's entitlements is extremely rare. Repealing a web of separate statutes is almost unprecedented—perhaps the only example is removing laws in the southern states on slavery and then, one hundred years later, on segregation.

This political giant emerged out of laws authorizing collective bargaining and an indifference to the overt conflict of interest by public employees organizing against the public interest. In little over a decade, teachers unions went "from somewhat sleepy organizations to ... the most powerful political forces in education."

The Political Resources of Public Unions

With an estimated seven million active members, public employee unions are far larger than other political interest groups.

Their reported contributions are among the largest of all interest groups. Terry Moe found that from 2000 to 2009, teachers unions "outspent all business groups combined" in thirty-six states. Total reported public union spending increased almost fourfold from the 2008 election to the 2020 election.

The reported union contributions, however, are the tip of a massive political iceberg. Most union political support is indirect, through campaign staff support, such as phone banks, and many other politically related activities and donations. While public unions keep their finances opaque, union revenues and political spending can be estimated within a general range and are multiples greater than reported contributions.

Public unions receive membership dues of about $5 billion each year—seven million active members pay dues of roughly $700 per year. Direct contributions to candidates and PACs, and payments to outside lobbyists, Daniel DiSalvo estimates, comprise at least 20 percent—about $1 billion per year, or $4 billion in each four-year election cycle.

But DiSalvo does not count union resources spent on self-directed political activity—including meeting with politicians and their staffs, public relations and advertising, campaign call banks, door-to-door canvassing, organized demonstrations with members and their families, providing senior staff for candidate campaigns, and recruiting and training union members to run for office. Michael Lilley of the American Enterprise Institute and Sunlight Policy Center unpeels the onion of teachers union activities in New Jersey and calculates that, from 2013 to 2017, $65 million per year, or "58 percent of total operational expenditures," was devoted to political activity. But even Lilley's estimate of actual spending is low, because it does not allocate any portion of massive union overhead to political activities.

Another way of assessing the union resources spent on political activity is to assess what unions do other than political action: i) They periodically negotiate collective bargaining agreements. ii) They also provide support for grievances and disciplinary proceedings but, for reasons noted, these are uncommon. DC 37, the AFSCME union in New York City, says it has sixty-five lawyers helping union members, which could conceivably cost 10 percent of its budget. iii) Unions offer training materials and incidental products such as discount cards, but these likely don't amount to much. Unions are also active in daily negotiations of on-site "union reps" with public supervisors and are conduits for supplemental health care and other benefits. But these are funded by government, not through union dues. The union reps are generally public employees and the supplemental benefits are "goodies" included in collective bargaining agreements (about $1.1 billion by New York City in 2018, allocated among almost one hundred union funds).

There is not much, in other words, that unions do with their revenues that is *not* political. It's hard to imagine that unions devote more than a third of their revenues to nonpolitical member services.

By these estimates, public unions spend somewhere between $1 billion and $3 billion each year to influence political decisions, or $4 to $12 billion in each four-year political cycle. No other interest group, no industry, comes close to mobilizing that amount of political money, particularly in state and local elections.

Scope of Union Political Influence

Public employee unions are a powerful force in national politics. About 10 percent of delegates to the Democratic National Convention are members of the teachers unions, "making them the single largest organizational bloc of Democratic Party activists."

In the unionized states, public unions are by far the preeminent influence in state and local races. Public unions' ability to "elect their own boss" is literally true—public unions are the mother's milk for state and local politicians. Daniel DiSalvo gives this example from California:

> The California Correctional Peace Officers Association (CCPOA) spent about $7 million on elections in the Golden State in 2010 … The CCPOA backed some 107 political candidates, 104 of whom won office. California State Senator Juan Vargas said, "I won by 22 votes and without

CCPOA it wouldn't have been close ... They literally won this campaign for me."

Each public union seems to operate out of the same playbook—to turn elected officials into union dependents.
"We elect our bosses, so we've got to elect politicians who
support us and hold those politicians accountable," as the
AFSCME website proclaims. Some unions have gone one
step further and gotten their own members elected. In
many states, teachers unions dominate school board elections, off-year events with low turnout where union members often run. A Michigan union brochure on getting
involved in school board elections had this title: "Electing
Your Own Employer, It's as Easy as 1, 2, 3."

The correlation of union support and election success,
Michael Hartney and others have found, is extremely
high: 70 percent of union-endorsed school board candidates win. What public unions ask in return is the rejec-
tion of most reforms, plus continual incremental controls
and benefits. Public unions do not get everything they
want, at least not immediately, but there is little organized opposition, and the steady drumbeat of pressure is
only in one direction.

Trying to reform union benefits and powers, political leaders soon learn, is playing with fire. While over
90 percent of union support goes to Democrats, even for
Republicans it's better just to steer clear of the dragon
guarding the cave of public administration. Complaining
about unions is far more prudent than actually taking

them on. The mouth of the dragon's cave is piled high
with the bodies of reformers.

Reform Is Bloody and Almost Always Unsuccessful.
New York City mayor Mike Bloomberg and his school
chancellor Joel Klein decided to pilot a new program
where the decision to grant tenure to new teachers would
be determined in part by the test scores of their students.
The union strongly opposed this but had no legal basis to
reject it. "In an awesome display of raw political power,"
Terry Moe reports, the union "went to the state legislature
in the spring of 2008 and got it to pass a law prohibiting
any district, anywhere in the state, from using test score
data as even one part of the tenure evaluation process."

Bold reformers soon learn that winning round one
generally attracts massive union reinforcements to
overturn the reforms. In 2007 Washington, DC, mayor
Adrian Fenty brought in Michelle Rhee as schools chancellor. Rhee closed schools that were failing, fired several
hundred teachers and principals—and instituted merit
pay. The teachers unions fought her at every step, but
her reforms seemed to be working and the unions were
unable to halt her progress. So the unions went to plan B
and "put the hard sell on" a council member to challenge
Mayor Fenty in the Democratic primary. The American
Federation of Teachers reportedly spent around $1 mil-
lion to unseat Fenty. Fenty lost, and Rhee resigned.

In 2011 Ohio governor John Kasich secured passage
of a law that limited collective bargaining to wages and

required public employees to contribute to pension and health-care benefits. The unions immediately sponsored a voter referendum to repeal the law. The unions built an astonishing war chest of $42 million from unions across the country to support the Ohio referendum and organized a get-out-the-vote campaign of a sort normally seen only in presidential elections. The all-unions-on-deck effort succeeded in reversing Governor Kasich's reforms.

The unions don't always win. They failed to unseat Florida governor Jeb Bush, who had instituted testing to evaluate teacher performance and supported voucher programs. But Governor Bush did not directly challenge union perquisites, as Rhee and Kasich had. Unions also failed to get President Obama to dismiss reform-minded Secretary of Education Arne Duncan.

The two notable victories over unions are remembered mainly for how bloody they were. In 1981 President Reagan broke the strike by air traffic controllers by firing over 11,000 of them and bringing in supervisors and military controllers to manage air traffic until new controllers were trained. In 2011, Wisconsin governor Scott Walker proposed a "budget repair bill" that required public employees to contribute to pension and health plans (reducing take-home pay by 8 percent), limited collective bargaining to wages (no more work rules, seniority, and other controls), and required public unions to be authorized by their members each year.

The unions went to war against Walker. They organized a massive demonstration of an estimated 100,000 people and physically occupied the state capitol. Protests of thousands of union employees were organized by unions in capitals across the country. To prevent a vote on the law, fourteen Democratic state senators left the state for several weeks to prevent a quorum. The proposed law did not apply to police or firefighters, but the threat of disruption and civil disobedience prompted Walker to put the National Guard on alert and to organize supervisors to perform essential services if public employees went on strike.

Walker stood his ground and secured passage of the law. The unions immediately sued and got a ruling declaring the new law invalid as violating state open-meeting laws. But the Wisconsin Supreme Court reversed. The unions then organized a recall petition to remove Walker from office and marshaled $18 million to get Walker removed. After another bloody campaign, Walker prevailed. The Milwaukee County district attorney, a Democrat, then commenced a criminal investigation on whether Walker had illegally coordinated with conservative groups engaged in issue advocacy in the recall election. This too went to the Wisconsin Supreme Court, which in 2015 held that "the special prosecutor's legal theory is unsupported in either reason or law."

Walker won. Once they lost their collective bargaining powers, the unions became a shadow of their former selves. In 2009, the year before Walker was elected, the Wisconsin Education Association Council employed seventeen lobbyists. By 2019, they had just two.

By most accounts, the reforms markedly improved Wisconsin's government and its economy. The state realized savings of $5 to $7 billion per year, some of which went into support of small business and tax reductions. An estimated 42,000 jobs were created. Schools improved—particularly math scores in nonurban schools and overall quality in school districts that instituted merit pay. Union membership declined from 50 percent to 22 percent of public employees. It appears as if even Democrats are happy to get unions off their backs. Schools and agencies are manageable and work better, and the state is no longer saddled with a large operating deficit.

Breaking union controls in Wisconsin required a kind of civil war, with four years of nonstop political and legal battles, and do not appear to be replicable in most states. Indeed, it appears that Walker was able to get elected initially only because, as the unions complained afterward, he disguised his intention to reform collective bargaining. Otherwise the unions would have gone to war earlier and made sure he wasn't elected.

The Union Political Party

Unions have organized themselves like a political party. Public employee unions do almost everything political parties do—including amassing huge war chests and thousands of campaign workers and using these resources to run candidates, oppose candidates, sponsor new laws, fight against reforms, and engage in public advocacy.

But the union party cannot boast of great public works or other clear accomplishments for the public good. It works only for its own benefit. Studies find that unions have the effect of increasing public spending, but not with corresponding public benefits. For example, Stanford economist Caroline Hoxby in 1996 found that teachers unions "succeed in raising school budgets and school inputs but have an over-all negative effect on student performance."

New Jersey teachers union: a case study of political power. How this works in practice is described in detail in a series of reports on the political activity of the New Jersey Education Association (NJEA) by Michael Lilley. With the notable exception of Newark and four other cities with high poverty and terrible schools, New Jersey has always had good schools. This is mainly because of demographics—New Jersey has a large cohort of highly educated, affluent parents, which is the common thread of other states with high-performing schools, such as Massachusetts, Connecticut, and Maryland. But instead of making New Jersey a peaceful island in America's education wars, the absence of crisis has emboldened NJEA to take command.

NJEA operates unmistakably like a political party, not an interest group:

—NJEA since the 1990s has had twenty field offices organizing political strategy and campaigns as well as working on local school issues. It does this through its organizing arm, UniServ, which is how, Michael

Lilley describes, "NJEA mobilizes its army of political 'volunteers' who contact legislators, turn out for rallies, staff campaigns, and otherwise provide the NJEA with its most powerful political weapon." NJEA president Dennis Testa put it this way: "Our dollar contribution isn't the deciding factor. We provide phone banks and phone calls and people who are willing to go door-to-door across the state."

—NJEA has its own Political Leadership Academy, which since 2011 has trained over fifteen hundred NJEA members to run for political office. The NJEA's rationale was clear: "It's no longer enough to elect friends of education to public office; we must elect members of the education family. No one in public office will speak up as strongly for public education as our own members ... It's no longer enough to lobby decision-makers. We must become decision-makers."

—In 2013 UniServ abandoned any pretense of separateness and moved into NJEA headquarters. At that point, nine of twelve senior NJEA executives were political organizers. In 2016 the union started a Summer Fellows Program, a "bold and unprecedented move to organize members" in political action. The union claims it turned forty-five thousand members into political activists.

Like an old-fashioned party boss, NJEA treats politicians like underlings. A politician's refusal to toe the union line results in immediate political retribution:

—In 1991, NJEA was angered by Democratic reforms to decentralize pensions to local school districts and to give tax relief to voters instead of increasing school funding. These relatively mundane policy differences were hardly the frontal assaults on union prerogatives waged by Scott Walker or Michelle Rhee. But union president Betty Kraemer took these decisions as a personal affront and said, "The Democratic Party must bear the responsibility." The union then put its campaign apparatus behind forty-six Republican candidates and threw Democrats out. "The result," Lilley reports, "was one of the most remarkable political coups in modern New Jersey history: a stunning Republican sweep." This palace coup resulted in a huge payoff over the next decade—not only repealing the pension shift but getting a 9 percent increase in pensions and premium-free health benefits for life for all members.

—By the 1990s, NJEA was largely in control of education policy. Education Commissioner Leo Klagholz in 1994 observed that the teachers union had become "the most powerful force in Trenton—not just in education, the most powerful force, period." Even with friends in the statehouse, NJEA was quick to pull out the union hammer. In 2006, when Governor Corzine called a special legislative session to deal with the pension crisis, NJEA organized a demonstration of 25,000 protesters wearing buttons that read, "In November, We'll Remember."

—NJEA was temporarily pushed back on its heels with the confluence of Governor Chris Christie, President Obama's Race to the Top initiative aimed at more school accountability, and the willingness of South Jersey Democrats, led by State Senate president Steve Sweeney, to impose testing and meaningful teacher evaluations. As with Michelle Rhee and John Kasich, NJEA began organizing how to undo the reforms in the next political cycle. In 2016 NJEA spent $5 million in a failed effort to unseat Senator Sweeney— probably the most money ever spent in America in a state legislative race.

—Equilibrium for NJEA was restored in 2016, when NJEA went all in for Democratic candidate for governor Phil Murphy "from day one, gearing up a massive organizing campaign to mobilize our members through the primary and general elections." The union Members4Murphy initiative "delivered 6,800 signatures to get Murphy on the Democratic primary ballot." As Michael Lilley reports, Members4Murphy "operated 20 phone banks, made 230,000 calls and conducted door-to-door canvasses … Near election day, members from all 21 counties 'went door-to-door, made phone calls, mailed postcards, and organized events to encourage members to support Murphy and other endorsed candidates.'"

Once Murphy won, NJEA got to work undoing Christie-era reforms. Murphy appointed the head of NJEA to lead his education transition team and another union official to be Murphy's deputy chief of staff. To keep public opinion quiescent, NJEA provided $10.5 million to the pro-Murphy New Direction New Jersey "dark money" nonprofit.

Here again, the payoffs were large. Policies championed by Governor Murphy include reducing teachers' health-care contributions, putting limits on school districts' ability to outsource educational support personnel (such as custodians and bus drivers), watering down teacher tenure rules, blocking pension reform, eliminating the new standardized tests, and advocating for a millionaire's tax to permit greater spending on the NJEA's priorities.

In 2018, the Supreme Court in *Janus v. AFSCME* barred unions from forcing nonunion employees to pay union agency fees. No problem for NJEA: in anticipation of the *Janus* ruling, Governor Murphy led passage of the Workplace Democracy Enhancement Act (WDEA), which gives NJEA exclusive access to new teachers on school property and exclusive control of their contact information, allows use of school email and communications, limits a teacher's ability to opt out of paying dues, and, best of all, makes the school liable for union dues if it discourages teachers from joining. The purpose and effect of WDEA is to pressure teachers to join the union while at the same time discouraging the school district or anyone else from informing teachers of their First Amendment rights.

NJEA has an annual revenue stream of an estimated $150 million, achieved through the authorization of collective bargaining and automatic "dues check off." It is incontrovertible that NJEA uses those resources politically to control education policy. The NEA and its state affiliates, such as NJEA, as the *New York Times* reported, are "organizations that once shunned political activity as incompatible with 'professionalism.'" Now they "have become one of the nation's most aggressive and effective political forces."

Who's in Charge?

Public employee unions act with a sense of entitlement that no other interest group can aspire to. Unions just say no to whatever they don't like. Even small reforms and accommodations in government are impossible without some sort of inducement. If an elected official or supervisor pushes too hard for a change, the threat of a strike or job action or political opposition is always a possibility. So who's really in charge?

At the beginning of 2022, almost two years after the COVID pandemic began, Chicago mayor Lori Lightfoot was still trying to cajole teachers unions to come back to schools. As Mayor Lightfoot put it, "They'd like to take over not only Chicago Public Schools, but take over running the city government."

Chapter 9:
What Were They Thinking?

*"The spirit of distrust of authority ... can be used
against the trustworthy too. An equal opportunity weapon,
it can be invoked by the misguided, the mendacious,
and the malevolent, as well as by the mistreated."*

—Robert A. Kagan

At this point, fifty years after public sector collective bargaining was authorized, it's hard to imagine that the original proponents intended anything like what happened. Revisiting their analysis reveals how unions took control of vital public choices in ways that the experts, based on their own analysis, would almost surely regard as unconstitutional.

The early forays into public sector collective bargaining—notably JFK's executive order 10988 in 1962—were not accompanied by meaningful analysis of how public sector bargaining would work in practice. By excluding compensation and other budgeting issues from bargaining, JFK's order also avoided a complete takeover of federal operations by unions.

The first large state to authorize collective bargaining, New York, did so after receiving a detailed report from an expert committee chaired by University of Pennsylvania law professor George Taylor. The 1966 Taylor Report did not dwell on the rationale for introducing public collective bargaining, other than this conclusory statement: "It is elementary justice to assure public employees, who are estopped from using the strike, that they have the right to negotiate collectively."

The Taylor Report dealt with several "serious pitfalls" in allowing what it called "collective negotiations" (to distinguish it from "collective bargaining" with trade unions). One concern was to avoid undermining New York's existing civil service system. The Civil Service Employees Association objected to union bargaining, noting that "fragmentation" of different bargaining units would destroy uniformity and cause "leapfrogging" of benefits—as each union sought a little more than the others. The Civil Service Employees Association was also concerned that the legislature would be influenced by union political power and would be unable to control what unions demanded. But the Taylor Report concluded it could avoid "undermining the Civil Service System" by "careful attention ... to defining the subject matter of joint negotiations."

The main concern of the Taylor Report was the need to retain political accountability over final union agreements:

It is ultimately the legislature and the political process which has to balance the interests of public
employees with the rest of the community, to re-
late the compensation of public employees to the
tax rate, and to appraise the extent and quality of
public services and the efficiency of their performance to the aspirations of public employees.

In the strongest terms, and repeatedly, the Taylor Report
rejected proposals for compulsory arbitration as both unlawful and an easy way to avoid responsibility:

There is serious doubt whether [compulsory arbi-
tration] would be legal because of the obligation
of the designated executive heads of government
departments or agencies not to delegate certain
fiscal and other duties ... The temptation in such
situations is simply to disagree and let the arbitrator decide.

In 1967 the New York State legislature enacted what became known as the Taylor Law, authorizing collective
bargaining while ignoring Taylor's strongest recommendation—to require that contracts be approved by the legislature. The Taylor Law was amended a few years later
to mandate compulsory arbitration for broad categories of
public safety employees and to allow voluntary agreements
for binding arbitration for all other employee categories.

Expert reports were also commissioned by at least
seven other states and the city of Los Angeles. Their
conclusions were generally similar to the Taylor Report,

for example, in rejecting compulsory arbitration for disputes and requiring legislative approval of final contracts. These reports also emphasized the need for public officials to retain "managerial prerogatives." For example, the report for Los Angeles stated,

> Managers of governmental agencies must insure that the functions intrusted to them are carried out promptly and without interruption. We think they should have the right initially to determine the manner in which these functions are to be performed ... unilaterally and without prior negotiation with employees or their organizations.

Yale Law labor expert Clyde Summers emphasized that public policy decisions, such as whether to "reduce classroom size" or to "provide police civilian review boards," should also be excluded from the scope of bargaining.

A critical mass of expert commentary also agreed that resolving labor issues by arbitration would be, as Professor Summers put it, "wrong in principle because the decisions to be made are political decisions ... [that] should be made through the political process in which voters have a voice." Arbitration would be an unlawful delegation of democratic power, allowing "public officials who should be responsible to evade that responsibility and push the decision off to an arbitrator."

Experts were less clear on why public sector collective bargaining was needed at all, after centuries without it. The prohibition against public strikes had long been in place in many jurisdictions and was toothless. Professor Summers came up with two justifications: first, that public employees were "massively outnumbered in votes" by citizens so that "collective bargaining enables them to offset this political disadvantage"; and, second, that "collective bargaining is necessary to protect employees against ... disagreeable working conditions and ... oppressive arbitrary action." Professor Summers gave no examples of either harm. Nor did he note that the civil service system had long afforded a wide range of protections to public employees.

In recent years, teachers unions have argued that unions were required because pregnant women were sometimes not allowed to teach, but that discriminatory practice was common throughout society, not just in schools, and largely ended by a Supreme Court ruling in 1974. No contemporaneous pro-union expert that I found referred to it as a rationale for bargaining.

The most commonly stated reason in the later 1960s was that public employees should have "rights ... similar to those accorded in the private sector." But there was also an undercurrent of fear. Nonrecognition of public collective bargaining, Yale Law professors Harry Wellington and Ralph Winter suggested, might also result in widespread labor strife:

> The danger to [the American political] process stems mainly from strikes. Although a policy of non-recognition seems to protect the political

process from public employee unions, it is ... not a realistic alternative. Non-recognition is too drastic, too plainly at odds with the premises of collective bargaining in the private sector.

What Could Go Wrong?

When compared with what actually happened, the experts had a perfect record of failure.

Instead of labor peace, collective bargaining in government incentivized labor leaders to go on strike. Labor lawyer Theodore Kheel in 1969 wrote that "it is probable that the Taylor Law exacerbated ... conflicts" by "encourage[ing] unions to threaten to strike to achieve the bargaining position participants in collective bargaining must possess." In the two years after passage of the Taylor Law, Kheel noted, New York had unprecedented labor strife:

In September 1967, the teachers in New York City struck for fourteen days. In the early hours of 1968 a transit strike was narrowly averted after negotiations under an implicit strike threat ... In February 1968, the sanitation service of New York City was interrupted for nine days, leaving the city unsightly, unkempt, infested with disease, plagued by the threat of fire, and seemingly helpless to correct the situation. And in the fall of 1968 the city's schools were closed for two months in a dispute that set new marks for bitterness and hostility, and raised spectres of racial and religious bias that threaten to undermine the fabric of social order.

Other important city workers, including police-
men and firemen, have either threatened strikes
or resorted to some form of job action.

New York was not alone. Strikes and threatened strikes
hit every state that authorized collective bargaining—
over four hundred strikes between the later 1960s and
1980. Strikes died down in the 1980s, probably not coin-
cidentally after public employee unions consolidated their
political and legal power. Strikes were no longer needed
to get what unions wanted at the bargaining table.

The expert recommendations of finely calibrating the
scope of bargaining and management prerogatives never
got anywhere. The unions took their seat of power and
immediately refused to go along with any policy, budgetary trade-off, efficiency, or other public decision that they
didn't like. As Jerry Wurf, the president of AFSCME, put
it, he now enjoyed "a power relationship where public
officials and policy makers respect you as equals and deal
with you."

Budgetary trade-offs by elected officials became a
matter not just of public policy, but of which union was
first in line. Democratic accountability was replaced in
many states by compulsory arbitration for key unions.

In a 1974 essay, Professor Sylvester Petro excoriated
the intellectual lemmings who rushed over the cliff of
public sector bargaining. The idea of co-government,
he noted, is a version of no government. Public budgets
are not abstractions but reflections of complex public

trade-offs. Requiring political leaders to appease each union, seriatim, diverts the focus from public goals to union consent. Daily governing choices are also impractical when an official must first satisfy the parochial interests of the union rep:

> Whenever a question arises, the two pass jointly upon all the minutiae of daily employment—hiring, firing, layoffs, changes in modes of production, work allocations, merit increases, subcontracting, and so on. When employer agents and union agents are unable to agree on the disposition of the matter in issue, under the usual collective agreement the issue is submitted to an arbitrator or to a board of arbitrators—again jointly chosen.

Sovereign power requires government authority to compel action, Petro explains, including "forc[ing] everyone to work for it," by taxation and other mandates. The elected leaders who are given this power are agents of the whole people and cannot relinquish it to anyone else. For that reason, Petro argues, sovereign legitimacy cannot survive ceding authority to unions. Empowering public unions to approve basic public choices, for their own benefit, "amounts to a voluntary forfeiture of its power to govern, and hence of its power to serve the whole community."

Why Nothing Changed

After passage of the collective bargaining laws in the late 1960s, the harms caused by union collective bargaining power were quickly apparent. Pandora's box had been opened, as one observer put it, and nothing but public ills poured out of it. Why didn't anyone do anything about it? In our democratic republic, lawmakers are supposedly able to repeal laws that don't work out.

Here as well, the architects of public collective bargaining failed to perceive how public bargaining would work in practice. What happened is that the interests of public unions and political leaders aligned to create a kind of bureaucratic kleptocracy. Campaign support plus bargaining power opened a wide door for mutual advantage.

The issue at the bargaining table is not whether to give unions at least some of what they want—that goes without saying in most negotiations—but how to moderate the demands and rationalize the result with the public. One easy way out is arbitration, which can be relied upon to give at least some of what unions demand: "The arbitrator made me do it." Another easy way of avoiding accountability is to embed benefits and restrictions in statutes: "The law made me do it."

Cornell professor Kurt Hanslowe, writing in 1967, predicted this new era of government by collusion:

> [Compulsory bargaining has] the potential of becoming a neat mutual back scratching mechanism, whereby public employee representatives and politicians each reinforce the other's interest and domain, with ... the individual citizen left to look on, while ... his tax rate and

> public policies generally are being decided by en-
> trenched … government officials and collective
> bargaining representatives over whom the public
> has diminishing control.

The prospect of citizens not represented at the bargaining table is why FDR adamantly opposed public sector
bargaining: "The employer is the whole people … Upon
employees in the Federal service rests the obligation to
serve the whole people …"

SECTION III:
Public Employee Controls
Are Unconstitutional

"In framing a government which is to be administered by men over men, the great difficulty lies in this: you must first enable the government to control the governed; and in the next place oblige it to control itself."

—James Madison

It is a basic principle of America's constitutional republic, applicable to state and local government, that government cannot delegate to private parties essential governing choices. "The power of governing is a trust committed by the people to the government," the Supreme Court held in *Stone v. Mississippi*, "no part of which can be granted away." Nor can a legislature remove the authority of future leaders to make the decisions "which, from the very nature of things, must 'vary with varying circumstances'":

> The people, in their sovereign capacity, have established their agencies for the preservation of the public health and the public morals, and the protection of public and private rights. These several agencies can govern according to their discretion, if within the scope of their general authority, while in power; but they cannot give away nor sell the discretion of those that are to come after them.

John Locke's Second Treatise is generally credited as the source of the "nondelegation principle": "The legislative cannot transfer the power of making laws to any other hands: for it being but a delegated power from the people, they who have it cannot pass it over to others."

As I will shortly argue, several specific provisions of the Constitution explicitly safeguard against the delegation of sovereign powers, including Article II and the Guarantee Clause in Article IV. But the core principle underlying these constitutional protections is the inviolability of sovereign power. Public union bargaining and political activity have supplanted or materially weakened sovereign power in at least four ways:

(i) Public bargaining disempowers elected executives. The ability of elected executives to manage government has been corroded beyond recognition by collective bargaining. Public unions have an effective veto over key operational decisions. As teachers union president Albert Shanker put it, "We have the power to stop a lot of things."

Sovereignty is corrupted if it is subject to another's approval. As an early Supreme Court decision put it, "Let a State be considered as subordinate to the people: but let everything else be subordinate to the State. The latter part of this position is equally necessary with the former." While collective bargaining doesn't give unions unilateral authority for whatever they want, it has allowed teachers unions, as a *New York Times* editorial put it, to seek "virtually total control over the schools."

(ii) Public sector bargaining preempts vital legislative responsibilities because it creates a powerful preference for union interests over other public interests. It puts union officials in "a power relationship," as union president Jerry Wurf put it, "where public officials and policy makers respect you as equals and deal with you."

But elected officials have a duty to "the whole people," as FDR put it, not just to employees represented by unions. That's why Professor George Taylor believed the legislature should approve each contract, and why other experts also sought to solve the nondelegation doctrine by limiting the scope of bargaining. Professor Clyde Summers explained,

> The collective agreement is not a private decision, but a governmental decision; it is not so much a contract as a legislative act. Labor costs may be seventy percent of a city's budget. Bargaining on wages and other economic items, therefore, inevitably involves the level of taxes and the level of services.

In a 1947 ruling, the Missouri Supreme Court explained why public sector bargaining necessarily preempts legislative responsibility:

> Under our form of government, public office or employment never has been and cannot become a matter of bargaining and contract ... This is true because the whole matter of qualifications, tenure, compensation and working conditions for any public service involves the exercise of legislative powers ... It is a familiar principle of constitutional law that the legislature cannot delegate its legislative powers and any attempted delegation thereof is void ... If such powers cannot be delegated, they surely cannot be bargained or contracted away.

(iii) When there is a bargaining impasse, in many states and in the federal government, unelected arbitrators are making legislative choices. New York State early on approved the role of arbitrators to "write collective bargaining agreements for the parties." But, as the Taylor Report in New York concluded, "There is serious doubt whether [compulsory arbitration] would be legal because of the obligation of the designated executive heads … not to delegate certain fiscal and other duties." A labor law treatise by Derek Bok and John Dunlop explained why:

> Arbitrators are seldom equipped to weigh the interests of government employees against the full array of claims on the public treasury. Legislators are elected in a democratic society to make such evaluations of the public welfare and priorities.

(iv) Sovereign authority is corroded by organized political activity by public unions. The resources of millions of public employees are aimed at changing public policy and compromising the constitutional authority of elected officials.

It is hard to reconcile organized public union political activity with the duty of loyalty owed by public employees. Just as public sector bargaining is different than trade union bargaining, so too political action by public employee unions is different than politics by other interest groups. The difference is ethical: Organizing politically against government to advance public employee self-interest is a breach of duty. This ethical conflict has constitutional proportions because union political power has enabled public servants, in complicity with elected officials, to disable the functioning of constitutional government.

In each of these four ways, public employee unions have subverted the sovereignty of government, broken the linkage to voters, and redirected public choices away from "promot[ing] the general welfare" to satisfying union demands.

In the 1973 *Letter Carriers* case, the Supreme Court addressed these potential harms when upholding the constitutionality of the Hatch Act, which bars political activity by public employees. While the holding addresses whether a specific statute is permissible, the reasoning of the decision reveals the constitutional imperative for a public service that is dedicated to the public good, not to benefiting itself:

> It seems fundamental in the first place that employees in the Executive Branch of the Government, or those working for any of its agencies, should administer the law in accordance with the will of Congress, rather than in accordance with their own or the will of a political party. They are expected to enforce the law and execute the programs of the Government without bias or favoritism for or against any political party or group or the members thereof.

The Court emphasized that public employees occupy positions of public trust and must not be seen to be partisan or self-interested:

> There is another consideration in this judgment: it is not only important that the Government and its employees in fact, avoid practicing political justice, but it is also critical that they appear to the public to be avoiding it, if confidence in the system of representative Government is not to be eroded to a disastrous extent.

Politicizing the public service into an organized bloc, the Court held, could upend democracy:

> Another major concern ... was the conviction that the rapidly expanding Government workforce should not be employed to build a powerful, invincible, and perhaps corrupt political machine ... using the thousands or hundreds of thousands of federal employees, paid for at public expense, to man its political structure and political campaigns.

The Court concludes that "the judgment of history" is that it is "essential" for public employment to "depend upon meritorious performance" and to limit public employees' "political influence":

> Such decision on our part would no more than confirm the judgment of history, a judgment made by this country over the last century that

it is in the best interest of the country, indeed essential, that federal service should depend upon meritorious performance rather than political service, and that the political influence of federal employees on others and on the electoral process should be limited.

Letter Carriers restates the core values of public loyalty and individual merit needed to govern modern society. In the recent *Janus and Knox* decisions, the Court noted the harmful effects of growing public employee union influence and invalidated state laws that allowed unions to draw agency fees from public employees who were not union members. It is now time to take the bull by the horns, removing public employee union controls and powers over American government.

America's constitutional republic is not structured to accommodate an outside power independent of the will of the people. The Constitution does not guarantee good government, of course. But it provides for a regular changing of the guard, through democratic elections, by which voters can pick new leaders with ideas on how better to "promote the general Welfare." The disempowerment of elected leaders by public employee unions has undermined this basic premise of constitutional government.

Chapter 10:
Restore Executive Power under Article II

*"Certain powers [are] in their nature executive,
and must be given to that depart[ment]."*

—James Madison

Article II of the Constitution provides, in its first sentence, that "the executive Power shall be vested in a President." The Supreme Court on many occasions has defined executive power, including the limits on Congress's authority to impinge on it.

The president and subordinate officials have only limited practical authority, as noted earlier, to manage public employees in unionized departments. That's partly because Congress, as part of broader reforms in the Civil Service Reform Act of 1978, codified earlier executive orders requiring the president to collectively bargain with the unions. All told, the executive branch must bargain with a dozen different unions, each focused on specific cohorts. Together 25 percent of federal employees belong to unions, with total coverage somewhat higher.

Nor can the president simply reject collective bargaining demands. Any dispute over a new collective bargaining agreement must be resolved by an independent Impasses Panel or an arbitrator selected by the Impasses Panel. In 2015, for example, the Veterans Administration wanted authority to assign personnel based on performance, not seniority. The union refused to agree, and the Impasses Panel required the VA to accept the union preference for seniority in the collective bargaining agreement.

Federal government, as noted, is an accountability-free zone. More federal employees die on the job than are terminated for poor performance. Regular stories emerge of employees who cannot be terminated despite outrageous behavior—such as the EPA employee who spent the day surfing porn sites. The head of the VA hospital in Phoenix, at the center of a 2014 scandal over falsified waiting times, was found not accountable for "lack of oversight" because, as Steven Brill recounts in *Tailspin*, the government failed to prove specific items of no oversight—overlooking the fact that oversight, by definition, is not limited to specific criteria. The IRS after two years finally removed an employee who systematically denied benefits to African immigrants, made repeated discriminatory remarks in the office, and tried to run another employee off the road. But the union lawyers who represented him required a clean personnel record as the quid pro quo for leaving, so he was soon spotted working for the US Forestry Service.

Nor can executive branch officials leave candid critiques in personnel files, at least not without advance notice and an opportunity to challenge the evaluation in a grievance proceeding. The legal process over a file comment can stretch out over months. That's why over 99 percent of federal employees receive a "fully success-ful" rating. The common thread in these proceedings is a legal presumption against crediting the supervisor's perceptions of who's doing the job and who's not.

Many daily management decisions are also subject to negotiation with the "union rep." For example, an office move at the Department of Energy was held up for months as the union rep insisted on approving each detail of who went where, who got windows, and how many square feet were allocated to different people. The National Treasury Employees Union agreement requires bargaining over use of any new technology—including new copy machines and software upgrades from, say, Outlook Desktop to Outlook 365. That agreement then requires a meeting within each working group of fifteen to twenty people to discuss the results of this bargaining.

Is it any wonder why good candidates are repelled by public service? All these union controls have not en-hanced the professional culture of federal civil service. Barely ten years after passage of the civil service reforms, the original Volcker National Commission on the Public Service in 1989 found that federal agencies suffer from "an erosion of performance and morale" and an "inability to recruit and retain a talented work force." The second Volcker Commission in 2003 found deep resentment at "the protection provided those poor performers among them who impede their own work and drag down the reputation of all government workers."

"I found that most people in my department wanted to be helpful," said Chad Hooper, a former IRS official who is now executive director of the Professional Managers Association. "But one person would bring down the morale of the entire team. All he needed to do is take days off during peak work times, and make flimsy excuses for not helping out. Pretty soon most other people would be discouraged."

The Partnership for Public Service in 2014 described the civil service controls as "a relic of a bygone era": "For managers, the process of removing or disciplining an employee is daunting in terms of the time and effort required, and often discourages managers from taking appropriate actions." The Senior Executive Association, representing an elite group of the most senior career officials, has repeatedly sought the authority to manage personnel. "It should not require an army of lawyers to effectuate a personnel action," said Jason Briefel, the association's director of government and public affairs. The difficulties in hiring and removal cause "a never-ending cycle of inefficiency and frustration."

The disempowerment of executive branch officials from making personnel decisions cannot be reconciled with the executive powers conferred by Article II of the Constitution. How well government works is part of the president's constitutional responsibility to "take care that the laws be faithfully executed." Managing government "as effectively and efficiently as possible" requires authority to manage public employees:

> Government employers, like private employers, need a significant degree of control over their employees' words and actions; without it, there would be little chance for the efficient provision of public services.

With limited exceptions, the scope of "executive power" must also include the authority to terminate officials. As the Supreme Court held in the *Free Enterprise Fund* case:

> The Constitution that makes the President accountable to the people for executing the laws also gives him the power to do so. That power includes, as a general matter, the authority to remove those who assist him in carrying out his duties. Without such power, the President could not be held fully accountable for discharging his own responsibilities; the buck would stop somewhere else. Such diffusion of authority "would greatly diminish the intended and necessary responsibility of the chief magistrate himself." (quoting Federalist 70)

As the drafters of the Pendleton Act understood when civil service was first proposed 150 years ago, Congress lacks the constitutional authority to take away the president's general powers over executive branch officers and employees.

There are two main restrictions on executive personnel power. The first was to protect against firing civil servants for partisan reasons. The Lloyd-LaFollette Act of 1912 allowed a complainant to appeal to the Civil Service Commission and to respond in writing, but no "examination of witnesses, trial, or hearing." The second restriction, originally set forth in *Humphrey's Executor* (1935), is that the president lacked that authority to terminate "*quasi*-legislative or *quasi*-judicial" officers, in that case a commissioner of the Federal Trade Commission, whose job requires them to act "independently of executive control." In those situations, the president must show "just cause" for removal.

In all other situations, the president and federal supervisory officials must have authority to manage personnel and make other operational decisions. This requires, among other remedies, invalidating specific provisions of the Civil Service Reform Act of 1978 that mandate collective bargaining, disempower the president and his appointees from removing officers, and require bargaining disputes to be resolved by the Impasses Panel.

Chapter 11:
Public Union Controls Undermine Democratic Governance

"It is one of the most prominent features of the Constitution, a principle that pervades the whole system, that there should be the highest possible degree of responsibility in all the Executive officers thereof; any thing, therefore, which tends to lessen this responsibility, is contrary to its spirit and intention."

—James Madison

A "republican form of government" is the keystone of American constitutional framework. The American republic, as noted, is structured to empower officials to act on their best judgment. That's why they're elected for fixed terms, so that they have sufficient room to make hard choices in the public interest without risking immediate recall. Through periodic choices at the ballot box, voters thereby maintain indirect control of how government works.

The American republic no longer works as designed because union controls disempower elected officials from managing government. Governors, mayors, and other public executives cannot remove these union controls because they are mandated by multiyear collective bargaining agreements and by statutes that can be removed only by legislatures. In addition to the nondelegation doctrine, there is also a specific constitutional provision under which executive disempowerment in state and local government should be ruled unconstitutional: the Guarantee Clause in Article IV of the Constitution.

The Guarantee Clause provides that the "United States shall guarantee to every state in this Union a Republican Form of Government." This provision forbids states from adopting any structure that might give operating control to an aristocracy or other permanent group, thereby breaking the linkage between voters and governing decisions.

The key characteristics of a "republican form of government," as described by James Madison in Federalist 39, are these:

> We may define a republic to be … a government which derives all its powers directly or indirectly from the great body of the people, and is administered by persons holding their offices during pleasure, for a limited period, or during good behavior. It is *essential* to such a government that it be derived from the great body of the society, not from … a favored class of it.

The evil that the Guarantee Clause protects against is a permanent power that is beyond the power of voters to remove. A republican form of government, Madison explained, precludes the takeover of the operations of government by "nobles" or other "favored class" who have not been "appointed, directly or indirectly, by the people":

> Otherwise a handful of tyrannical nobles, exercising their oppressions by a delegation of their powers, might aspire to the rank of republicans, and claim for their government the honorable title of republic. It is *sufficient* for such a government that the persons administering it be appointed, either directly or indirectly, by the people; and that they hold their appointments by ... [their] tenures.

Voters today elect public executives who promise reform but cannot override union controls to change how government operates. Public unions have become a permanent faction exercising control over the operating machinery of state and local governments.

America's history has provided only a few occasions to invoke the Guarantee Clause. Abraham Lincoln invoked the Guarantee Clause to justify opposing secession. According to historian William Wiecek, "Lincoln reasoned that if a state may secede, it may discard the Republican form." Abolitionists had long invoked the clause to challenge slavery.

On the few occasions where the Guarantee Clause has been presented to the Supreme Court as the basis for judicial relief, the Court has held that the clause is "non-justiciable," meaning it should be enforced by political branches, not by courts. Thus, in an 1849 case, the Supreme Court declined to decide whether a state constitution written by a dissident group of Rhode Island citizens was more "republican" than the existing constitution. In a 1912 case, the Court refused to adjudicate whether a citizen referendum was a republican form of government, emphasizing the political nature of the dispute.

In *Baker v. Carr*, the 1962 decision where the Supreme Court enshrined the principle of "one man, one vote," Justice Brennan reviews those precedents and concludes that, while not applicable in *Baker*, the Guarantee Clause could be judicially enforceable in cases that do not involve "political questions":

> [The] Guaranty Clause claims involve those elements which define a 'political question,' and for that reason and no other, they are nonjusticiable ... [T]he nonjusticiability of such claims has nothing to do with their touching upon matters of state governmental organization.

Recent political questions that the Court has refused to decide include gerrymandering, where parties draw electoral district lines to benefit themselves. Whether or not these lines are fair, the Court held, are matters of policy that should be decided by partisan politics.

Here, by contrast, union controls of the operating machinery of government are structural, not political.

While unions use political power to acquire these controls, preserving the management authority of officials is essential to our constitutional structure. What's at stake is not the wisdom of a partisan policy, but whether elected officials have the authority to fulfill their constitutional responsibilities—say, to terminate an ineffective teacher or an abusive cop. Supervisory authority is an operational imperative for democratic accountability to voters.

The constitutional error of union controls is compounded, in many jurisdictions, by the requirement to submit bargaining disputes to arbitrators. Arbitrators, elected by no one, make legislative judgments about critical public trade-offs and operating mechanisms.

When the city of Buffalo objected to a proposed 10 percent raise for police, the impasse was resolved by an arbitration panel, which granted a 5 percent increase. When Buffalo objected that it could not afford the increase, the arbitrators made a legislative decision:

> The fiscal problems of the City must be weighed against the services performed by a police officer... Buffalo police officers can surely be asked to share in this fight, but can't be expected to bear the full burden of the City's fiscal problems.

A police pay raise in Buffalo may or may not have been prudent. What was required was a governing judgment, weighing which other services must be cut—say, frequency of trash collection, or school athletic programs—or measuring the impact of tax increases. That governing judgment must be made by elected officials accountable to voters, not by unelected arbitrators. Nor does voluntary arbitration resolve the nondelegation problem. Elected officials have the job of making these trade-offs, not punting tough choices to arbitrators. "Private arbitration of public-sector disputes," Professor Petro concluded, is an "obviously unconstitutional delegation of legislative power."

By severing the linkage between the ballot box and executive and legislative powers, public unions have disabled the "Republican Form of Government" guaranteed by the Constitution. Americans no longer enjoy, to quote Madison, "a government which derives all its powers directly or indirectly from the great body of the people." Instead, the operations of government have come under the control of a "favored class" that is not accountable to the people or their elected representatives.

These union controls are embedded in contracts and statutes that new executive leaders have no legal authority to change. In these circumstances, the Guarantee Clause should be judicially enforced to remove collective bargaining and other shackles on executive and legislative authority.

Chapter 12:
Public Service Is a Public Trust, not a Political Party

"Most evil is done by people who never make up their minds to be good or evil."

—Hannah Arendt

Political organizing by public sector unions is assumed to be lawful because the First Amendment allows everyone else to organize politically. But public employees, unlike all outside interest groups, have an ethical responsibility to serve the public, not negotiate against it. Moreover, union political organization is aimed at influencing the political leaders with whom unions are bargaining. Public employees use political power to skew and sometimes corrupt constitutional government, to their own benefit and almost always to the harm of the public.

For these reasons, organized political activity by public employee unions should be ruled unconstitutional. Public employees individually will still be free to engage in political activity and expression, but not to mobilize the resources of, literally, millions of public employees against the public good.

Public Employees Owe Fiduciary Duties to the Public.

The Constitution is permeated with the goal of serving the public good, for example, to "promote the general Welfare." Laws must be "necessary and proper" and "be faithfully executed." The president must "take care" to fulfill executive responsibilities.

Article VI requires that "all executive and judicial Officers, both of the United States and of the several States, shall be bound by Oath or Affirmation, to support this Constitution." Public employees' duty of loyalty is also explicitly set forth in federal regulations for all federal employees:

> *Public service is a public trust.* Each employee has a
> responsibility to the United States Government
> and its citizens to place loyalty to the Constitution,
> laws and ethical principles above private gain.

This duty of public employees is fiduciary, according to ethicist Hana Callaghan, meaning the public employee has an "obligation to put the public's interest before their own direct or indirect personal interests." Because government has a monopoly on essential services, enforced with sovereign power, citizens are at risk in public dealings. Fiduciary duty serves as a higher standard for public accountability.

While the scope of fiduciary duty varies with the responsibility, acts taken by public employees to harm the public and benefit themselves will always be a breach of duty. As stated in one Supreme Court decision,

> [The policeman is] entirely responsible to the city or State which is his employer. He owes his entire loyalty to it. He has no other 'client' or principal. He is a trustee of the public interest, bearing the burden of great and total responsibility to his public employer.

One of the founders of the labor movement in the late nineteenth century, Samuel Gompers, refused to let police join his union because he felt police would have a divided loyalty between duties to the public and union ties to striking workers.

The line between ethical and unethical activity is often drawn where there are divided loyalties. For private trade unions, the NLRA does not allow managerial employees to unionize because of "divided loyalties." Unlike private sector workers, almost all public employees owe enhanced fiduciary loyalties as agents of the state. Police have coercive powers, teachers provide essential services, inspectors oversee health and safety, and transit repair crews keep the trains running. Their enhanced duty of loyalty to the public good, as FDR emphasized, is the main reason why they were excluded from the NLRA.

Public employees are still entitled to represent their personal interests, for example, in fair compensation. A public employee should be allowed, as this ethical guidance in Massachusetts states, to "represent his own personal interests ... on the same terms and conditions that would apply to other similarly situated members of the public."

Political organizing by public unions is not aimed at a public employee's "own personal interests," however, but at changing and controlling public policy. The "divided loyalty" of public unions is more accurately described as a breach of public trust. To review the bidding:

—Instead of promoting excellence, public unions prevent accountability of abusive cops, inept teachers, and ineffective public employees.

—Union work rules are designed for inefficiency and avoiding merit—for example, padding of job crews with featherbedding and make-work requirements, prohibitions on pitching in, and seniority over quality.

—Union pension rules are written to be gamed against the public interest—for example, spiking of overtime to enable pensioners to inflate the pensions.

—Massive political donations and support are distributed so that elected leaders answer to unions, not voters.

While the constitutional propriety of public unions organizing politically has not been directly challenged, the Supreme Court has repeatedly held that the right of public employees to express their views does not extend to matters affecting their job. The duty of public employees is to provide public services "as effectively and efficiently as possible." That's why, as noted earlier, "Government employers, like private employers, need a significant degree of control over their employees' words and actions."

Nor can public employees avoid their ethical responsibilities by delegating antisocial activities to their unions. Unions, as agents for their members, are bound by employees' ethical obligations.

Corrupting Constitutional Government

The Constitution embodies a presumption that public employees work for the public. As the Supreme Court noted in upholding the Hatch Act,

> It seems fundamental in the first place that employees in the Executive Branch of the Government, or those working for any of its agencies, should administer the law in accordance with the will of Congress, rather than in accordance with their own or the will of a political party. They are expected to enforce the law and execute the programs of the Government without bias or favoritism for or against any political party or group or the members thereof.

The conflict between nonpartisan public service and organized union political activity is unavoidable. What are they organizing for? "The political orientation of public-sector unions," Professor Petro observed, "constitutes a radical contradiction of the basic objective of civil-service merit systems: insulation of public servants from external political forces, to the end that the sovereign government serves faithfully, without corruption and discrimination, all the people."

The union goal is to elect pliable officials who will support the union agenda. In the 2012 *Knox* case, addressing union political assessments, the Supreme Court quotes fliers from the SEIU "Political Fight-Back Fund" discussing how "public worker unions are in the process of raising the extraordinary funds needed to defeat the Governor." Campaign funds must be raised, the union flier continues, "to elect a governor and a legislature who support public employees."

What would be illegal in a trade union bargaining— for management under the table to induce the cooperation of friendly workers—is standard practice in public sector bargaining, except reversed: The political nature of decisions allows public unions to influence elected officials who are supposed to be representing the whole people. By "increasing use of campaign contributions ... to public officials with whom the union will be negotiating," as labor lawyer Theodore Clark predicted, public unions "sit on both sides of the bargaining table."

What corrupts democracy is not the idea of unions— it's not hard to imagine unions that actually promote better schools and greater efficiency. Prior to collective bargaining, the National Education Association was a professional association that eschewed politics and promoted best practices in schools. Over 75 percent of public employees in Denmark and Canada are unionized, but the bargaining in those countries does not impinge on normal managerial prerogatives. Denmark has a "flexicurity" program that allows workers to be easily terminated, providing instead for up to two years of income support. Instead of rigid work rules, Denmark and most unionized countries have workers' councils that address workplace issues. The critical distinction in those countries, however, is that unions there are not negotiating with their political dependents. In Canada, there are significant limits on election-related spending. In Denmark, the officials with the responsibility to bargain with unions are not politically elected or appointed. Unions lobby for labor-friendly policies, but they don't have their thumb on the scale.

The corrosive effect of organized union political activity was highlighted in the 2018 *Janus* case, where the Supreme Court declared unconstitutional an Illinois state statute that required public employees who were not union members to contribute agency fees. The basis for the decision was that compelling agency fees was "forced speech" violating the First Amendment—that nonmembers were forced to fund political positions with which they might not agree. The Court's opinion goes further, however, and describes social damage resulting from the growth of public union power:

> This ascendance of public-sector unions has been marked by a parallel increase in public spending ... Not all that increase can be attributed to

public-sector unions, of course, but the mount-
ing costs of public-employee wages, benefits, and
pensions undoubtedly played a substantial role.
We are told, for example, that Illinois' pension
funds are underfunded by $129 billion as a result
of generous public-employee retirement packages. Unsustainable collective bargaining agreements have also been blamed for multiple municipal bankruptcies.

In Illinois, the Court noted, a "'quarter of the budget is
now devoted to paying down' … unfunded pension and
retiree healthcare liabilities," and yet unions prevented
elected officials from tightening the belt:

> But when the State offered cost-saving proposals
> on these issues, the Union countered with very
> different suggestions. Among other things, it ad-
> vocated wage and tax increases, cutting spend-
> ing "to Wall Street financial institutions," and …
> closing "corporate tax loopholes," "[e]xpanding
> the base of the state sales tax," and "allowing an
> income tax that is adjusted in accordance with
> ability to pay."

Janus observes that public unions also exercise their influence on how government operates. In schools, for example, unions are involved in managerial policy:

> Should teacher pay be based on seniority, the
> better to retain experienced teachers? Or should
> schools adopt merit-pay systems to encourage

teachers to get the best results out of their students? Should districts transfer more experienced teachers to the lower performing schools that may have the greatest need for their skills, or should those teachers be allowed to stay where they have put down roots? Should teachers be given tenure protection and, if so, under what conditions? On what grounds and pursuant to what procedures should teachers be subject to discipline or dismissal? How should teacher performance and student progress be measured—by standardized tests or other means?

Janus offers these examples as showing how "[s]peech in this area also touches on fundamental questions of education policy." What's actually happened in schools, however, is not merely political speech by public unions, but political control by unions. Each of the Court's questions about school policy, for example, have long since been dictated by public unions.

Crafting a Constitutional Cure

At this point, public unions are entrenched as political kingmakers. While ending public sector collective bargaining will re-empower elected executives, it is unlikely to resolve the political conflict of interest. Even states that do not permit collective bargaining find that their politics are skewed by public union political power.

The question presented is this: Should public unions be able to mobilize the resources of millions of public employees, in breach of their duties of loyalty, to achieve a veto over government operations? The Supreme Court has no obvious doctrine that protects against organized public employee disloyalty. The Court has used the First Amendment to try to defend good government from unnecessary partisan influence—including barring patronage firings and ending union agency fees. But the First Amendment can't cure the corruption of a conflict of interest.

Constitutional government cannot withstand the organized political power of public employees who, in breach of their fiduciary duties, demand policies that harm the public. Watching public employee unions organize in the late 1960s, Professor Kurt Hanslowe predicted that democracy itself would be the loser: "There are limits on the amount of stress which a democratic government can tolerate from organized group pressure. At some point its fibre can be broken, and democratic rule under law be replaced by authoritarian rule by clique."

Political activity by public unions should be ruled unconstitutional. The Supreme Court need not create a broad loyalty doctrine. It needs only to hold that organized political activity by public employees involves an unavoidable conflict of interest with the core values of the Constitution: that officials should aspire to "promote the general welfare" with "necessary and proper" laws and "take Care that the Laws be faithfully executed."

Chapter 13:
Abolish the Union Spoils System

"We are determined to respect everyone but we have forgotten that respect has to be earned....It is our reluctance to make demands on each other...that is sapping the strength of democracy."

—Christopher Lasch

In 1983 the National Commission on Excellence in Education released "A Nation at Risk," a report on declining achievement in America's schools. Its recommendations included a longer school year, rigor in grading and expectations, and accountability for ineffective teachers. The report struck a nerve and touched off reform initiatives around the country. Twenty-five years later, a follow-up report sponsored by the Rockefeller, Broad, and Gates Foundations found that "stunningly few of the Commission's recommendations" had been enacted. The problem was not ideas: "We have enough commonsense ideas, backed by decades of research, to significantly improve American schools." The problem was political: "State and local leaders have tried to enact reforms ... only to be stymied by organized special interests and political inertia."

Democracy no longer works because public unions have turned the constitutional hierarchy upside down. America's republican form of government is aimed at electing officials who are accountable to voters. Instead, because of the rise of public union power, officials are accountable to public employees. The path to union power was collective bargaining. As Michael Hartney explains in *How Policies Make Interest Groups*, collective bargaining was the vehicle for organizing the resources of millions of public employees into billions of campaign funds.

What happened is in plain sight: Public unions have created a modern spoils system. Just as the spoils system ran government for the benefit of campaign supporters of the winning party, public unions control government operations for the benefit of public employees. Like the old Tammany machine in New York, public unions have consolidated their political might to advance policies aimed at keeping public employment as a sinecure, unmanageable and unreformable.

But union controls are far more destructive of democracy because they're permanent. Public union entrenchment doesn't change with the new party in power. At least the old spoils system had crude episodic accountability. The union spoils system, by contrast, is encased in legal entitlements and powers and, as Professor Petro observed, is never directly put to the vote:

> They are ... active at every level of political activ-
> ity—lobbying, testimonial dinners for candidates,
> financial contributions, registration drives, vast
> mailing campaigns, political brochures, etc. But
> they are not openly and candidly a political par-
> ty; they never expose their policies to the test of
> the secret ballot for the approval or disapproval
> of the general electorate.

The insidious nature of union controls is that they make government work badly while also preventing reform. Just as light through a lens is transformed into a beam that burns, union powers focused only on government operations have burned through the connecting links between officials and voters. By severing the cord to voters, government operations in many states have drifted away from public purpose, from political control, and from the verdict of the public supposedly served.

Reclaiming Public Purpose

Government works only when dedicated to its public purpose. Federal experts every day confront threats of domestic terrorism, cyberwarfare, adulterated food and drugs, international fraud, overfished oceans, and much more. At the state and local level, many cops, teachers, inspectors, road crews, and others provide essential services for our communities. Find any public department that is effective, and you will also find public employees focused on achieving public goals.

Public trust also requires a public service that aspires to be noble, not self-seeking. Creating something greater than yourself is a natural human aspiration. The nobility of public service is on display during times of crisis. When the contagious, life-threatening Ebola virus began to endanger entire populations in West Africa in 2014, the Centers for Disease Control in Atlanta asked for volunteers to go there to try to help contain the spread. Two thousand federal employees volunteered. During the COVID pandemic, the advice of public health officials was at the top of the news every day. They proved not to be infallible, but we still looked to them for guidance as the evidence kept changing.

Honorable public service has one essential condition: dedication to the public purpose. Loyalty to the greater good is what earns public servants their honor:

> Civil servants bear special responsibilities for the public. They exercise public powers on behalf of the country. They spend public money for important government projects. They raise taxes. They hunt down criminals. They protect the people. They take decisions which have an impact on the fundamental rights of citizens. They decide on health and on risk protection ... For all these important tasks, it is important that the public servants exercise their role properly, and act lawfully, honestly and loyally without acquiring any personal advantage.

That description of public service comes from the European Institute for Public Administration.

The prevailing value in American public service today, at least in unionized states and departments, is entitlement, not dedication to public purpose. Cynicism has replaced loyalty. The 1989 Volcker Commission found that seven out of ten federal employees who witnessed fraud, waste, or abuse did not even bother to report it. Police are conditioned to obey a "code of silence," not stop abuse when they see it. Good teachers quit because of the dispiriting cultures of their schools.

Selfishness is probably the most corrosive value in any organization. When people get away with not trying hard, and taking sick days when they're not sick, and gaming the system for higher pensions, the effect on work culture is lethal.

Public employee unions in America are engines of selfishness—partisan machines dedicated to their own self-interest. They demand entitlements, rigidities, compensation gimmicks, public policies with no public benefit, and veto rights on public management, and do so holding elected leaders at political gunpoint. "Everything is about jobs," as former California Senate majority leader Gloria Romero put it. Union officials "walk around [the capitol] like they're God."

It is perhaps no coincidence that the United States ranks twenty-seventh in World Bank ratings on government effectiveness. Public trust is also low—near the bottom of OECD developed countries.

What does it take to make American government work better? There are a thousand ways to improve government, but each of those ways must meet the litmus test of dedication to the public good. As FDR put it, "Government is competent when all who compose it work as trustees for the whole people."

It is impossible to have good government without a culture of shared public purpose. Every good school, every good public department, has a culture of shared commitment. Culture is far more important than structure or strategy. "Culture eats strategy," as the management theorist Peter Drucker put it.

"The key is pride," air force general and head of the Strategic Air Command Bill Creech observed. "Pride is the fuel of human accomplishment, so you've got to give people something to be proud of."

A public culture dedicated to the common good unleashes human energy and innovation. "No one has a greater asset," management expert Mary Parker Follett observed, "than a man's pride in his work."

But pride must be earned to be real. Happy talk about pride doesn't work if the school is lousy or the department tolerates slackers. Only people who work hard, and see others similarly committed, and deliver services as well as they can, will feel genuine pride.

How can a cynical, moribund organization be transformed into one that makes its employees proud? The second Volcker report called for "far-reaching changes in the structure and operations of the federal government." Overhauling public operations will require re-empowering people to take responsibility. Leaders must be empowered to make changes and enforce values of public purpose. Public employees at all levels must have a sense of ownership of the choices they make.

Change is hard in the best of circumstances, and especially when the culture has been corrupted with an entitlement mentality, hardened into bureaucratic defensiveness. The safe route today is to avoid responsibility, not take responsibility. The Ten Commandments of Government, according to one public administration expert, are these: "Thou shalt not make a mistake. Thou shalt not make a mistake. Thou shalt not make a mistake ..."

Some public employees will not accept, much less embrace, a new culture focused on public results. They're comfortable with routine and entitlement. Change will be impossible unless leaders are empowered to let people go. "If resistance is tolerated," public management experts David Osborne and Peter Plastrik explain in *Banishing Bureaucracy*, "then maybe the leader isn't really serious about change. It poisons the atmosphere for those who do take on the difficult transition to a new culture." Quoting air force general Michael Loh, they conclude that "the best policy is to give people one chance, then move them out."

All roads to honorable public service lead back to accountability. Culture change is impossible without accountability. Sustaining a good culture is impossible unless accountability is a realistic possibility. "You don't have to fire all the resisters," Osborne and Plastrik note, "only a few. The others will see you are serious and either get on board or take one of your exit routes."

Good Government: Purpose, Power, and Accountability

The Constitution is our lodestar here. Its governing structure is designed for elected officials to exercise independent judgment for the public interest. It allocates powers so that officials have authority to make needed decisions.

Union controls are built on the opposite assumption— that official authority is a suspect category. Everything about the union premise is wrong. How is it that a public employee has rights superior to a public supervisor? Who's looking out for the public interest? What about the rights of coworkers, the rights of the public supposedly being served, and the rights of voters who are choosing who can best deliver public services?

Reviving executive power is not a danger to good government, but indispensable. Public leaders are like hubs on a wheel. They must be empowered to make trade-offs, try new approaches, and coordinate public employees and public resources. Unions have disconnected the spokes. For any new situation, the spokes clang about, and the department goes nowhere until the union decides whether and on what terms it will move forward.

The abject failure of governing without executive power is undeniable. Treating every personnel decision as a crime against nature, instead of fostering a utopia of perfect fairness, has bred a moldy culture that consigns public employees to dreary workplaces without pride and camaraderie. The dismemberment of authority repels good candidates by precluding what makes public service fulfilling—the chance to make a difference.

The union narrative plucks a sensitive string in the American psyche: distrust of authority. The framers, too, confronted this distrust. They resolved it not by disempowering officials but by empowering other officials to act as checks and balances. Providing checks to authority is the correct model, not ceding controls to self-interested unions.

No one elected unions to co-run American government. No democratic principle gave legislators and other officials the right to surrender governing powers to unions. No ethical value allows public employees, having taken an oath to protect the public, to organize politically to harm the public. Democracy under union restraints can't work as the framers intended. That's why union controls on the operating machinery of government should be ruled unconstitutional.

Notes

Introduction

7   **Derek Chauvin:** See, e.g., Derek Hawkins, "Officer Charged in George Floyd's Death Used Fatal Force Before and Had History of Complaints," *Washington Post*, May 29, 2020.

    See Labor Agreement Between the City of Minneapolis and the Police Officers' Federation of Minneapolis (2017–2019), on file with author. These impediments to management were not abstract. "For years in Minneapolis," Mayor Jacob Frey said shortly after Floyd's death, "police chiefs and elected officials committed to change have been thwarted by police union protections and laws that severely limit accountability among police departments." (Jessie Van Berkel and Liz Navratil, "Minnesota Human Rights Department Launches Probe Into Minneapolis Police," *Star Tribune* [Minneapolis], June 3, 2020). Then Minneapolis police chief Medaria Arradondo argued in June 2020, "There is nothing more debilitating to a chief than when you have grounds to terminate an officer for misconduct and you're dealing with a third-party mechanism that not only allows for that employee to be back in your department, but to be patrolling in your communities." (Douglas Belkin, Kris Maher, and Deanna Paul, "Clout of Minneapolis Police Union Boss Reflects National Trend," *Wall Street Journal*, July 7, 2020.) Tony Bouza, Minneapolis's police chief from 1980 to 1989, was more colorful in describing his lack of authority: "I was never able to fire the alcoholics, psychos and criminals in the ranks." (Belkin, Maher, and Paul, "Clout of Minneapolis Police Union Boss").

7   **"A social organism of any sort whatever":** William James, "The Will to Believe," in *Pragmatism and Other Writings*, ed. Giles Gunn (New York: Penguin Classics, 2000), 214.

8   **Twenty-six hundred complaints:** Dan Frosch et al., "The Minneapolis Police Chief Promised Change. He Got a Disaster," *Wall Street Journal*, May 31, 2020.

8   **a school principal in New York:** Susan Edelman, "Queens Principal
     Booted for Fraud Will Get Nice Paycheck for 7 Years," *New York Post*,
     April 16, 2022: "Under Abdul-Mutakabbir, Maspeth HS created fake
     classes, awarded credits to failing students, and fixed grades to push kids
     out the door."

8   **An EPA employee:** Employee Misconduct at the U.S. Environmental
     Protection Agency, Before the Committee on Oversight and Govern-
     ment Reform, U.S. House of Representatives, 114th Cong. (2015) (State-
     ment of Patrick Sullivan, assistant inspector general for investigations,
     Office of Inspector General, U.S. Environmental Protection Agency.)

9   **A New York City Parks Department employee:** Daniel DiSalvo,
     Government Against Itself: Public Union Power and Its Consequences (New York:
     Oxford University Press, 2015), 192–93.

9   **"on average public service delivery":** David Osborne and Ted Gae-
     bler, *Reinventing Government: How the Entrepreneurial Spirit Is Transforming the
     Public Sector* (New York: Plume, 1993), 81.

9   **Rigid job categories:** Interview by author with former official from the
     Metropolitan Transportation Authority.

10   **High school graduation rates:** Douglas N. Harris and Matthew F.
     Larsen, "Taken by Storm: The Effects of Hurricane Katrina on Me-
     dium-Term Student Outcomes in New Orleans," Education Research
     Alliance for New Orleans, July 15, 2018, updated May 17, 2021, 3–6,
     22, 52.

10   **a female painter:** DiSalvo, *Government Against Itself,* 25–26.

12   **Democratic Assemblyman Daniel Newman:** Mike Lilley, "'And
     You Will Pay': How a Special Interest Dominates New Jersey Politics,"
     American Enterprise Institute, October 2017, 6.

SECTION I: UNIONS AGAINST DEMOCRACY

Chapter 1: Why Nothing Much Gets Fixed

18   **The plague of public powerlessness:** See generally Philip K.
     Howard, *The Rule of Nobody: Saving America from Dead Laws and Broken
     Government* (New York: W. W. Norton, 2014) and Philip K. Howard,
     The Death of Common Sense: How Law Is Suffocating America (New York:
     Random House, 1995).

21   **"exclusive and illimitable power of removal":** Free Enterprise
     Fund v. Public Company Accounting Oversight Board, 561 U.S. 477,
     493 (2010).

21   **"exclusive and illimitable power of removal":** CSC v. Letter Carriers, 413 U.S. 548, 565 (1973).

Chapter 2: How Public Employee Unions Seized Control of Public Administration

25   **"How can one expect":** Polybius, *The Histories*, trans. Mortimer Chambers (New York: Washington Square Press, 1966), 226.

25   **a report by New Dealer Jim Landis:** James M. Landis, Report on Regulatory Agencies to the President-Elect (Washington, DC: US Government Printing Office, 1960).

26   **"impossible to bargain collectively":** George Meany, "Meany Looks at Labor's Future," *New York Times Magazine*, December 4, 1955, 38.

26   **"Meticulous attention should be paid":** Franklin D. Roosevelt to Luther C. Steward, August 16, 1937, from the American Presidency Project.

26   **Ending the spoils systems:** Daniel DiSalvo, *Government Against Itself: Public Union Power and Its Consequences* (New York: Oxford University Press, 2015), 44–46.

27   **Teddy Roosevelt in 1902:** Executive Order 163 of January 31, 1902.

27   **"political activity":** An Act to Prevent Pernicious Political Activities ("Hatch Act"), Pub. L. 76–252 (codified as amended in scattered sections of 5 U.S.C.).

27   **"break the back":** DiSalvo, *Government Against Itself*, 48–49.

27   **"efficient administration of the Government":** Executive Order 10988 of January 17, 1962, 27 Fed. Reg. 551; see DiSalvo, *Government Against Itself*, 48–50. The recommendation to authorize collective bargaining was set forth in a report by Arthur Goldberg to the president. The "Employee-Management Cooperation in the Federal Service" report is noteworthy mainly for its lack of substance—conclusory statements about the many benefits of public collective bargaining without factual or analytical support.

27   **the actual motivation was political:** DiSalvo, *Government Against Itself*, 49.

27   **National headlines were made:** See, e.g., "Teachers in Utah Set 2-Day Strike," *New York Times*, May 17, 1964; Sydney H. Schanberg, "Welfare Strike Is Unresolved; Union Chiefs Cheered in Jail," *New York Times*, January 23, 1965; "Strict Rules Set on Travel Into the City During Strike," *New York Times*, January 1, 1966; Jerry M. Flint, "Detroit Police Call End to Slowdown," *New York Times*, June 21, 1967.

28   **The independent Taylor Committee:** "Governor's Committee on Public Employee Relations: Final Report," March 31, 1966, 39–40.

28   **the New York legislature:** Public Employees' Fair Employment Act of 1967 ("the Taylor Law"), Consolidated Laws of New York, Chapter 7, Article 14.

28   **the second Taylor Committee:** "Governor's Committee on Public Employee Relations: Interim Report," June 17, 1968, 10.

28   **"The only illegal strike":** Associated Press, "Air Traffic Controllers Set a June 22 Strike Deadline," *New York Times*, May 24, 1981. Robert Poli was the renegade head of the Professional Air Traffic Controllers Organization who in 1981 went on to eat his words by leading perhaps the most famous unsuccessful public employees strike—resulting in President Ronald Reagan firing over eleven thousand air traffic controllers.

28   **thirteen states:** William H. Holley, Jr., Kenneth M. Jennings, and Roger S. Wolters, "The Labor Relations Process" (Mason, Ohio: South-Western, 2012), 577.

28   **Chicago mayor Richard Daley:** DiSalvo, *Government Against Itself*, 51.

28   **Thirty-eight states authorized collective bargaining:** A total of twenty-four states (Alaska, California, Connecticut, Delaware, Florida, Hawaii, Illinois, Massachusetts, Maine, Michigan, Minnesota, Missouri, Montana, Nebraska, New Hampshire, New Jersey, Nevada, New York, Ohio, Oregon, Pennsylvania, Rhode Island, Vermont, Washington) and the District of Columbia have a general authorization of public sector collective bargaining via either enacted legislation or case law compelling collective bargaining for a majority of public sector employees across most if not all of the state. An additional thirteen states (Alabama, Colorado, Iowa, Idaho, Indiana, Kansas, Kentucky, Maryland, North Dakota, New Mexico, Oklahoma, South Dakota, Utah, West Virginia) have a partial authorization of collective bargaining and either merely permit but do not require collective bargaining for a majority of public sector employees or otherwise limit the occupations, jurisdictions, or terms of bargaining covered. In the remaining thirteen states (Arkansas, Arizona, Georgia, Louisiana, Mississippi, North Carolina, South Carolina, Tennessee, Texas, Virginia, Wisconsin, Wyoming) public sector collective bargaining is weak or nonexistent, as it is either explicitly banned or otherwise significantly restricted.

27   **about seven million active public employees:** U.S. Department of Labor, Bureau of Labor Statistics, Union Membership (Annual) News Release, Released January 20, 2022.

29 **The two teachers unions:** Unless otherwise indicated, union membership was based on "Form LM-2 Labor Organization Annual Report 2021" filings, U.S. Department of Labor, Office of Labor-Management Standards, Public Disclosure Room. The AFSCME, AFGE, and NTEU numbers include retirees. The SEIU's Form LM-2 does not distinguish between public and private sector members, so we rely on their website. The American Postal Workers Union (APWU) has two hundred and twenty-three thousand public sector members, but, because the postal service operates like a business, the bargaining dynamics are similar to those of trade unions, and the analysis here is not applicable.

29 **35 percent of public employees:** U.S. Department of Labor, Bureau of Labor Statistics, Union Membership (Annual) News Release, Released January 20, 2022; Barry T. Hirsch and David A. Macpherson, Union Membership and Coverage Database from the Current Population Survey: Note, *Industrial and Labor Relations Review*, Vol. 56, No. 2, January 2003, 349–54 (updated annually at unionstats.com). Public sector union density in individual states is calculated based on the results of the Current Population (CPS) Outgoing Rotation Group (ORG) Earnings Files: California: 54.5 percent, Connecticut: 68.3 percent, Illinois: 48.7 percent, Minnesota: 54.7 percent, New Jersey: 59.3 percent, New York: 66.7 percent, Oregon: 57.7 percent, Pennsylvania: 53.3 percent, and Rhode Island: 66.6 percent.

30 **"difficult to make":** Joel Seidman, State Legislation on Collective Bargaining by Public Employees, 22 LAB. L.J. 13, 21–22 (1971), discussed in Sylvester Petro, "Sovereignty and Compulsory Public-Sector Bargaining," 10 *Wake Forest L. Rev.* 25, 50 (1974).

30 **"salient differences":** Russell A. Smith, "State and Local Advisory Reports on Public Employment Labor Legislation: A Comparative Analysis," 67 *Mich. L. Rev.* 891, 896 (1969).

30 **"In private employment":** Clyde W. Summers, "Public Employee Bargaining: A Political Perspective," 83 *Yale L.J.* 1156 (1974).

30 **"We have the ability":** Victor Gotbaum, as quoted in "Captive Politicians," *New York Times*, July 9, 1975.

34 **the vocational program was abandoned:** Charles M. Rehmus, "Constraints on Local Governments in Public Employee Bargaining," 67 *Mich. L. R.* 919, 919–20 (1969).

34 **"Collective bargaining is premised on":** R. Theodore Clark Jr., "Politics and Public Employee Unionism: Some Recommendations for an Emerging Problem," 44 *U. CIN. L. REV.* 680, 684 (1975).

35   **"we are a force to be reckoned with"**: Eric Katz, "Federal Employee Union Vows to 'Open a Can of Whoop Ass' on Unfriendly Lawmakers," *Government Executive*, February 9, 2015.

35   **"We helped get you into office"**: DiSalvo, *Government Against
Itself*, 81.

35   **"in effect, sit on both sides"**: Clark, "Politics and Public Employee
Unionism," 684.

35   **an "impassioned" New Jersey governor Jon Corzine**: DiSalvo, *Government Against Itself*, 57. "Such stories are not atypical," DiSalvo
writes. "The powerful Speaker of the New York State Assembly, Sheldon
Silver, once told the United Federation of Teachers at a rally that: 'I and
my colleagues in the Assembly majority will be your best friends … in
Albany.'" DiSalvo, Government Against Itself, 57–58.

36   **"In order for an institution"**: Petro, "Sovereignty," 66. See also 101:
"Government services stand outside the market. They are ruled essentially
by political values and considerations rather than by the cost-accounting
and other economic considerations … This applies to *all* government
services. It makes no difference whether we are talking about the police, the fire department, the schools, the military, the public parks, or
garbage collection, or municipal transit systems. None is run for a profit. The budget for each is the product of a political, not an economic,
process. That political process goes by the name of popular sovereignty.
Ultimately, the voting public decides through its elected representatives
how much money should be apportioned …"

36   **"irreconcilable conflict"**: Petro, "Sovereignty," 26.

37   **"plunged into municipal treasuries"**: DiSalvo, *Government Against
Itself*, 55.

37   **Accountability became virtually impossible:** See discussion in
Chapter 4.

37   **two or three per year:** See Vergara v. State, 202 *Cal. Rptr.* 3d 262
(2016); George F. Will, "The Injustice of California's Teacher Tenure,"
Washington Post, July 13, 2016.

37   **Work rules became an exercise in micromanagement:** See discussion in Chapter 5.

38   **Public benefits became progressively richer:** See discussion in
Chapter 6.

38   **"Unlike unions in the private sector"**: DiSalvo, *Government Against
Itself*, 34.

39   **Political activity:** See discussion in Chapter 8.

Chapter 3: How Public Employment Is Supposed to Work

41   **"At every stage of the governmental hierarchy":** Friedrich A. Hayek, *The Constitution of Liberty*, ed. Ronald Hamowy (Chicago: University of Chicago Press, 2011), 213.

42   **"each department should have":** James Madison, "Federalist no. 51," in Alexander Hamilton, John Jay, and James Madison, *The Federalist Papers*, (Project Gutenberg Etext, 1998).

43   **"chain of dependence":** Annals of Congress, 1st Cong., 1st sess., 518.

43   **Economist Mark Zupan:** Mark A. Zupan, *Inside Job: How Government Insiders Subvert the Public Interest* (New York: Cambridge University Press, 2017), 22–26.

43   **over fifty lifetime judicial appointments:** See, e.g., Kathryn Turner, "The Midnight Judges," U*niversity of Pennsylvania Law Review* 109 (1961).

44   **replace the spoils system:** See discussion in Philip K. Howard, "From Progressivism to Paralysis," 130 *Yale L. J.* (2021) and Philip K. Howard, *Try Common Sense: Replacing the Failed Ideologies of Right and Left* (New York: W. W. Norton, 2019), 98–102.

44   **"did not restrict the President's general power":** Gerald Frug, "Does the Constitution Prevent the Discharge of Civil Service Employees?" 124 *University of Pennsylvania Law Review* 942 (1976), 955.

44   **"Administration lies outside":** Woodrow Wilson, *The Study of Administration*, 2 Pol. Sci. Q. 197, 210 (1887).

44   **"skill, ability, fidelity, zeal and integrity":** Daniel DiSalvo, *Engines of Change: Party Factions in American Politics*, 1868–2010 (New York: Oxford University Press), 2012, 160 (quoting Cong. Globe, 39th Cong., 2d. Sess. 838–39 [1867]).

44   **"tak[ing] any part in the business of electioneering":** *Biography of an Ideal: The History of the Federal Civil Service, Office of Personnel Management* (Washington, DC, 1998), 12.

45   **"if the front door":** George William Curtis, president, National Civil-Service Reform League, National Civil-Service Reform League, Address at the Annual Meeting of the National Civil-Service Reform League (Aug. 1, 1883), in *Proceedings at the Annual Meeting of the National Civil Service Reform League* 3, 24–25.

45   **The new civil service system:** See discussion in Philip K. Howard, "From Progressivism to Paralysis," 130 *Yale L. J.* (2021) and Philip K.

Howard, *Try Common Sense: Replacing the Failed Ideologies of Right and Left* (New York: W. W. Norton, 2019), 98–102.

46   **"merely that the executive":** Gerald E. Frug, "Does the Constitution Prevent the Discharge of Civil Service Employees," 124 *U. Pa. L. Rev.* 942, 956 (1976).

46   **Harry Hopkins had hired 2.6 million unemployed Americans:** Harold Meyerson, "Work History," *American Prospect*, May 2, 2010.

46   **"Government is a human institution":** Report of the President's Committee on Administrative Management (Washington, DC: US Government Printing Office, 1937), 65.

SECTION II: PUBLIC EMPLOYEE UNIONS AGAINST THE COMMON GOOD: A FIVE-POINT INDICTMENT

47   **"A government ill executed":** Alexander Hamilton, "Federalist no. 70," in Alexander Hamilton, John Jay, and James Madison, *The Federalist Papers*, (Project Gutenberg Etext, 1998).

49   **"constitutional need":** Garcetti v. Ceballos, 547 U.S. 410, 445 (2006) (Breyer, J., dissenting).

Chapter 4: No Accountability

51   **"People we rated 'outstanding'":** Testimony of James B. King, hearing before Subcommittee on Civil Service, Committee on Government Reform and Oversight, House of Representatives (October 12, 13, and 25, 1995), p. 57.

51   **"Any government":** Paul Volcker, "The Endangered Civil Service," *New York Times*, August 5, 1990.

51   **Economist Eric Hanushek:** Eric A. Hanushek, "The Economic Value of Higher Teacher Quality," *Economics of Education Review* 30 (2011), 466.

52   **Reuters compiled a report:** Reade Levinson, "Across the U.S., Police Contracts Shield Officers from Scrutiny and Discipline," Reuters, January 13, 2017.

52   **A 2017 *Washington Post* report:** Kimbriell Kelly, Wesley Lowery, and Steven Rich, "Fired/Rehired," *Washington Post*, August 3, 2017,

52   **overturned by arbitrators:** See, e.g., Stephen Rushin, "Police Arbitration," *Vanderbilt Law Review* 74 (2021), 1030.

52   **over 70 percent of San Antonio police officers:** Rushin, "Police Arbitration," 1045.

52 **a small fraction of 1 percent:** See, e.g., Kellie Lunney, "Firing Federal Employees Isn't Easy, But It Can Be Done," *Government Executive* (May 29, 2014) (showing that fewer than ten thousand federal employees out of 2.1 million were fired for cause in 2013).

52 **About 0.2 percent of Connecticut public employees:** Marc E. Fitch, "Permanent Employees: Only .2 Percent of State Employees Terminated for Work Performance Issues," The Yankee Institute, March 15, 2021.

52 **In the private sector:** See, e.g., Bureau of Labor Statistics, "Annual Total Separations Rates by Industry and Region," March 10, 2022.

53 **"eight teachers":** Terry M. Moe, *Special Interest: Teachers Unions and America's Public Schools* (Washington, DC: Brookings Institution Press, 2011), 187.

53 **Illinois was even worse:** Moe, *Special Interest*, 186.

53 **"Dismissing a tenured teacher is not a process":** Amita Sharma, "Tenure: A Double-Edged Sword for 80 Years," *Santa Cruz Sentinel*, April 8, 1999, A1, A8.

53 **in one hearing observed by journalist Steven Brill:** Steven Brill, *Tailspin: The People and Forces Behind America's Fifty-Year Fall—and Those Fighting to Reverse It* (New York: Knopf, 2018), 265–66.

53 **the procedural trip wires:** See, e.g., Stephen Rushin, "Police Union Contracts," *Duke Law Review* 66 (March 2017).

54 **"performance improvement plan":** 5 C.F.R. § 432.

54 **The National Treasury Employees Union collective bargaining agreement:** Internal Revenue Service and National Treasury Employees Union, 2019 National Agreement, (2019), 123–24.

54 **"I'm here to defend":** Allison Pries, "Teacher Union President Suspended After Allegedly Saying 'I'm Here to Defend Even the Worst People,'" NJ.com, May 3, 2018.

54 **"If I'm representing them":** Moe, *Special Interest*, 185.

55 **"If we assume":** Moe, *Special Interest*, 184–185.

56 **"WEBEHWYG":** Mark A. Abramson and Paul R. Lawrence, eds., *Learning the Ropes: Insights for Political Appointees* (Lanham, Maryland: Rowman & Littlefield Publishers, 2005), 47.

56 **Just give a workers' committee:** See discussion in Philip K. Howard, *Try Common Sense: Replacing the Failed Ideologies of Right and Left* (New York: W. W. Norton, 2019), 102–04.

56   **the *availability of accountability***: See discussion in Howard, *Try Common Sense*, 90–93.

Chapter 5: Unmanageable Government

59   **"I need some of my management rights back"**: Daniel DiSalvo, *Government Against Itself: Public Union Power and Its Consequences* (New York: Oxford University Press, 2015), 183.

59   **The traits of effective teachers:** See discussion in Philip K. Howard, *Life Without Lawyers: Restoring Responsibility in America* (New York: W. W. Norton, 2010), 93–121.

59   **Policing requires instincts:** See, e.g., Michael Lipsky, *Street-Level Bureaucracy: Dilemmas of the Individual in Public Service* (New York: Russell Sage Foundation, 2010).

60   **digging a hole for a pole:** Chester I. Barnard, *The Functions of the Executive* (Cambridge, Massachusetts: Harvard University Press, 1968), 197–98.

60   **"It is one of the most prominent features of the Constitution":** James Madison, speech in Congress on the Removal Power, May 19, 1789, in *Writings* 435 (ed. Jack N. Rakove, 1999).

60   **"Nothing that's any good":** Neil Baldwin, Edison: *Inventing the Century* (Chicago: University of Chicago Press, 2001), 296.

61   **"If the contract were all about wages and benefits":** Daniel DiSalvo, *Government Against Itself: Public Union Power and Its Consequences* (New York: Oxford University Press, 2015), 198.

61   **"no one was manning":** Courtney Gross, "Crisis on Rikers Island: Hundreds of Officers Out Sick," NY1.com, May 16, 2022.

61   **"Virtually any idea for saving money":** E. J. McMahon and Terry O'Neil, "Taylor Made: The Cost and Consequences of New York's Public-Sector Labor Laws," Empire Center, May 2018.

62   **"that excellent teachers":** Moe, *Special Interest*, 4.

62   **the Sacramento teacher of the year:** Daniel Macht, "'Teacher of the Year' Axed in Budget Cuts," NBC Bay Area, June 15, 2012.

62   **even though studies:** Moe, *Special Interest*, 180

62   **"an extraordinary document":** Joel Klein, "Scenes From the New York Education Wars," *Wall Street Journal*, May 10, 2011.

63   **"It's too bad":** Moe, *Special Interest*, 174.

63   **"Rules that require principals":** Moe, *Special Interest*, 175.

64 **"Who in their right mind":** Moe, *Special Interest*, 4.

64 **One rookie teacher I interviewed:** See discussion in Philip K. Howard, *The Collapse of the Common Good: How America's Lawsuit Culture Undermines Our Freedom* (New York: Ballantine Books, 2002), 94–95.

65 **"There is no breakfast duty":** See discussion in Howard, *The Collapse of the Common Good*, 123.

65 **One report in Seattle:** Moe, *Special Interest*, 183.

65 **paint up to ten feet:** Eva Moskowitz, "Breakdown," *Education Next*, June 22, 2006.

65 **In another incident:** See discussion in Howard, *The Collapse of the Common Good*, 96.

65 ***The Prize:*** Dale Russakoff, *The Prize: Who's in Charge of America's Schools?* (New York: Houghton Mifflin Harcourt, 2015), 36–37, 135–138, 215–18.

66 **"The more restrictive the contract":** Moe, *Special Interest*, 212.

66 **Ignore the rules:** See discussion in Howard, *Life Without Lawyers*, 93–121.

67 **When former Indianapolis mayor Stephen Goldsmith:** See discussion in Philip K. Howard, *The Rule of Nobody: Saving America from Dead Laws and Broken Government* (New York: W. W. Norton, 2014), 109.

67 **Garbage collection in New York:** Citizens Budget Commission, "Getting the Fiscal Waste Out of Solid Waste Collection in New York City," September 23, 2014. See also Aaron Short, "New York Is Top of the Heap in Garbage-Hauling Costs," *New York Post*, May 24, 2014.

67 **"the garbage truck routes":** DiSalvo, *Government Against Itself*, 208.

67 **engineers on the Long Island Railroad:** Alfonso A. Castillo, "LIRR's Archaic Work Rules Prove Costly," *Newsday*, September 19, 2011.

68 **A series of articles on LIRR work practices:** See, e.g., Nicole Gelinas, "Here's How the LIRR Union Contracts Send Overtime Soaring," *New York Post*, May 5, 2019; *Newsday*, "A look at LIRR union work rules," September 17, 2011; Castillo, "LIRR's Archaic Work Rules Prove Costly." See also Carrie H. Cohen, "Report of Findings and Recommendations for the Metropolitan Transportation Authority, Overtime Policies and Procedures," August 15, 2019: "Arcane collective bargaining agreement … provisions and work rules, which often lack any modern justification, constrain management's ability to assign work in the most cost-efficient manner, and inflate overtime costs, including the worst instances by authorizing workers to be paid for hours they did not actually work."

69   **"until we get the virus under control":** Frederick M. Hess and Hayley Boling, "Are Teachers Unions Overplaying Their Hands?" *The Dispatch*, July 31, 2020.

69   **most public schools remained closed:** See, e.g., Michael B. Henderson, Paul E. Peterson, and Martin R. West, "Pandemic Parent Survey Finds Perverse Pattern: Students Are More Likely to Be Attending School in Person Where COVID Is Spreading More Rapidly," *Education Next* 21, no. 2 (Spring 2021) (found that only 24 percent of public schools had reopened for in-person learning by the end of the fall 2020 term compared to over 60 percent of parochial or private schools).

69   **"[The Los Angeles union imposed]":** Hess and Boling, "Are Teachers Unions Overplaying Their Hands?"

70   **columnist Jonathan Chait reports:** Jonathan Chait, "Zero COVID Risk Is the Wrong Standard," *New York*, March 3, 2021, and Chait, "The Madness of Teachers Unions Opposing a Vaccine Mandate," *New York*, August 3, 2021.

70   **"learning loss":** Chait, "The Madness of Teachers Unions Opposing a Vaccine Mandate."

70   **"Vaccinations must be negotiated":** Chait, "The Madness of Teachers Unions Opposing a Vaccine Mandate."

Chapter 6: Unaffordable Benefits, Hidden from Taxpayers and Paid by Our Children

71   **"The ultimate question":** Victoria J. Barnett, *"After Ten Years:" Dietrich Bonhoeffer and Our Times*, (Minneapolis: Fortress Press, 2017), 15.

72   **Teacher pay in some states:** For instance, in some rural Pennsylvania districts, starting teachers make less than $19,000 a year. See, National Education Association, 2019–2020 Teacher Salary Benchmark Report, April 26, 2021.

72   **Unfunded benefit liabilities:** See, e.g., the Pew Charitable Trusts, "The Challenge of Meeting Detroit's Pension Promises," March 2018.

72   **"every penny":** Hunter Walker, "Mayor Bloomberg Launches Coalition to Back Pension Reform With TV Ad Blitz," *The Observer*, May 13, 2012.

72   **A 2021 Moody's report:** Noah Shaar, "S&P: Growing Debt, Refusing Reforms, Population Loss Doom Illinois Pensions," Illinois Policy Institute, August 11, 2021.

72 **A study by the Urban Institute:** Richard W. Johnson, C. Eugene Steuerle and Caleb Quakenbush, "State Pension Reforms: Are New Workers Paying for Past Mistakes?" Urban Institute, July 2012.

73 **Some observers have suggested that bankruptcy:** See, e.g., David A. Skeel, "States of Bankruptcy," 79 U. Chi. L. Rev. 677 (2012).

73 **Des Moines cut library hours:** Daniel DiSalvo, *Government Against Itself: Public Union Power and Its Consequences* (New York: Oxford University Press, 2015), 176.

73 **Rockford, Illinois, may soon sell:** Adam Schuster, "Rockford Sees Public Pension Eat Nearly 40% of Municipal Property Taxes," Illinois Policy Institute, September 16, 2021.

73 **Pasadena cut over 120 local jobs:** Anita Yadavalli, "How Cities Around the Country Address Rising Pension Liabilities," National League of Cities (2018).

73 **Oakland in 2010 laid off eighty police officers:** Matthai Kuruvila, "Oakland Talks Break Down: Layoffs for 80 Cops," *San Francisco Gate*, July 14, 2010.

73 **The bottom line:** See, e.g., Rhode Island Public Expenditure Council, "Private Sector vs. Public Sector Compensation—A Preliminary Comparison of Salary and Benefits in Rhode Island," November 2011 (finding that public sector employer contributions to health-care and retirement benefits significantly outstripped contributions in the private sector).

73 **"Health and pension benefits":** Sarah Anzia and Terry Moe, "Public Sector Unions and the Cost of Government," *The Journal of Politics* 77, no. 1 (January 2015), 116.

74 **"The basic process by which states":** Jeffrey Dorfman, "Illinois Credit Downgrade Proves Public Pensions Should Be Outlawed," *Forbes*, June 5, 2017.

75 **economist Mark Zupan calls "slack":** See, e.g., Joseph Kalt and Mark Zupan, "The Apparent Ideological Behavior of Legislators: Testing for Principal-Agent Slack in Political Institutions," *The Journal of Law and Economics* 33, no. 1 (April 1990).

75 **How is it that 40,000 public employees:** Wayne Winegarden, "Reforming Public-Sector Pensions to Improve California's Fiscal Outlook," Pacific Research Institute, September 2018.

75 **In Illinois:** Jake Griffin, "Illinois Six-Figure Pensions Grow 74% Since 2015," *Daily Herald*, July 1, 2019.

75 **In many cities and states:** See, e.g., Jessica Boehm, "Arizona Supreme Court Says Phoenix City Employees Must Stop 'Pension Spiking,'" *Arizona Republic*, July 10, 2020.

75 **Under collective bargaining agreements:** See, e.g., Richard W. Johnson and Owen Haage, "Evaluating Pension Reform Options with the Public Pension Simulator: A Case Study of Pennsylvania Teachers," Urban Institute, March 2017 (describing how teachers can retire with full pensions in their fifties).

75 **California allows many state workers:** DiSalvo, *Government Against Itself*, 31. For a fuller discussion of California employees' rich retirement benefits, see Steven Greenhut, *Plunder!: How Public Employee Unions Are Raiding Treasuries, Controlling Our Lives, and Bankrupting the Nation* (Santa Ana, California: The Forum Press, 2009), 24-70.

75 **Police, firefighters, and other public safety employees:** See, e.g., National Conference of State Legislators, "State Retirement Plans for Public Safety Workers—Tables," August 2012; City of Orlando, "Police Pension Fund Participants' Retirement Options."

76 **Within the next fifteen years:** Liz Farmer, "As Retirees Outnumber Employees, Pensions Seek Saviors," *Governing*, September 2015.

76 **Retiring with full benefits ten years early:** Retiring ten years early at age fifty-five results in present value cost to the employer that is about 250 percent greater than the same person working another ten years and then retiring at half pension, based on these assumptions: Retire ten years early i) at half pension, ii) without continuing to contribute 8 percent to pension for those ten years, iii) receiving health-care benefits worth $10,000 annually for those ten years, until Medicare kicks in, and iv) at a 4.5 percent discount rate. See also Johnson and Haage, "Evaluating Pension Reform Options."

76 *Eighty percent* **of New Jersey sheriffs:** Mark Lagerkvist, "New Jersey Voters Can't Change Double-Dippers with Elections," *New Jersey Watchdog*, October 25, 2013.

76 **Almost 10 percent of Oregon's public employees:** Ted Sickinger, "Oregon PERS: About 1 In 10 Pensioners Are Rehired, Draw a Second Public Paycheck," *The Oregonian*, April 29, 2012.

76 **the village official in Illinois:** Patrick Hunzer, "Oak Brook Mayor, Wife, Collect $142k From 4 Pensions," *Chicago Daily Herald* (January 12, 2011).

76 **"Chief's Disease":** San Francisco Civil Grand Jury, "Pensions: Beyond Our Ability to Pay," (2009), 4. See also Greenhut, *Plunder!*, 57-60.

77 **"unexpectedly large increases":** Dan Goldhaber, Cyrus Grout, and Kristian Holden, "A Method for Identifying Salary Spiking: An Assessment of Pensionable Compensation and Reform in Illinois," National Center for Analysis of Longitudinal Data in Education Research, working paper, June 2020.

77 **Long Island Railroad chief measurement operator Thomas Caputo:** See, e.g., Nolan Hicks, Elizabeth Rosner, and Ruth Brown, "MTA's Top Earner Made $344K in Overtime Last Year," *New York Post*, April 23, 2019. According to a press release from the Department of Justice detailing Caputo's sentencing, he was able to collect so much overtime in part because, as an employee with significant seniority, the union contract made him eligible for whatever voluntary overtime shifts he wanted. "Highest Paid MTA Employee in 2018 Sentenced to 8 Months in Overtime Fraud Scheme," U.S. Attorney's Office, Southern District of New York, February 4, 2022.

In the 2000s, upwards of 97 percent of LIRR employees were retiring with disability, entitling them to additional retirement funds, even though virtually none of them had any disability while actually on the job. This disability rate "def[ied] medical explanation," especially since many so-called disabled workers were regulars at Long Island's Sunken Meadow golf course. After a *New York Times* investigation, the $1 billion "Gravy Train" scam was eventually broken up, resulting in jail time for several participants. See, e.g., Walt Bogdanich, "A Disability Epidemic Among a Railroad's Retirees," New York Times, September 20, 2008.

77 **a fire chief in Contra Costa County, California:** Nowicki v. Contra Costa County Employees Retirement Association, 67 *Cal. App.* 5th 736 (2021).

77 **a police lieutenant:** San Francisco Civil Grand Jury, "Pensions," 4.

77 **The 2020 Illinois report:** Goldhaber, Grout, and Holden, "Salary Spiking," 7.

78 **In the private sector:** Bureau of Labor Statistics, "Employee Benefits in the United States," March 2021, Table 3.

78 **According to the National Conference of State Legislatures:** National Conference of State Legislatures, "State Employee Health Benefits, Insurance, and Costs," May 1, 2020.

78 **In New York City:** City of New York Office of Labor Relations, "New York City Summary Program Description: Health Benefits Program," March 2022.

78 **If NYC employees contributed only 10 percent:** See, e.g., Barbara Caress, "New York City Overpays for Health Insurance. City Workers

Still Get a Bad Deal," the New School Center for New York City Affairs, January 20, 2021 (showing that NYC spends over $8 billion annually on current employee health-care costs). This figure only includes current employees and retirees under sixty-five; adding in the additional $3 billion the city spends on retiree health care would drive the savings figure up to over $1 billion. See, e.g., Peter Warren, "New York's Growing Debt Iceberg," Empire Center, November 1, 2021.

78   **New York City in 2021:** Editorial Board, "Saving the Savings: City Shouldn't Give Up on Medicare Advantage Plan After Legal Setback," *New York Daily News*, March 6, 2022.

79   **In a 2013 paper:** Thom Reilly, "Comparing Public-Versus-Private Sector Pay and Benefits: Examining Lifetime Compensation," 42 *Pub. Personnel Mgmt.* 521, 531–36 (2013).

79   **"employees of all levels of government":** Philipp Bewerunge and Harvey S. Rosen, "Wages, Pensions, and Public-Private Sector Compensation Differentials," Princeton University, Griswold Center for Economic Policy Studies, working paper No. 227 (June 2012), 21–22, 27.

79   **In New Jersey, for example:** Mike Lilley, *Job Number One: The New Jersey Education Association's Role in New Jersey's Disastrous Pension and Benefits Crisis*, American Enterprise Institute, 2017, 10–11, 14.

80   **"no longer within the State's means":** New Jersey Pension and Health Benefit Study Commission, "Supplemental Report on Health Benefits," February 11, 2016.

80   **Five years after the report was published:** New Jersey Department of the Treasury, "Statutory Funding Status: Pension Fund Actuarial Liabilities and Assets," July 1, 2020.

Chapter 7: Public Policy Against the Public Interest

83   **"We have produced politics by a hidden elite":** Fareed Zakaria, *The Future of Freedom: Illiberal Democracy at Home and Abroad* (New York: W. W. Norton, 2007), 198.

83   **the Citizens Budget Commission:** Andrew S. Rein, president, Citizens Budget Commission to New York State governor Kathy Hochul, "CBC Urges Veto of 21 Benefit Sweeteners," October 4, 2021.

84   **the California Correctional Peace Officers Association:** Joshua Page, *The Toughest Beat: Politics, Punishment, and the Prison Officers Union in California* (New York: Oxford University Press, 2013), 111–136.

84   **One person was sentenced:** David Kohn, "Three Strikes," *60 Minutes II*, CBS News, October 28, 2002.

84 **the California state prison population:** Legislative Analyst's Office, California State Legislature, "How Many Prison Inmates Are There in California?" January 2019.

84 **So did the number of CCPOA members:** Page, *The Toughest Beat*, 48.

84 **So did the compensation of prison guards:** Daniel DiSalvo, *Government Against Itself: Public Union Power and Its Consequences* (New York: Oxford University Press, 2015), 159.

84 **Correctional Officers Bill of Rights:** Charles Lane, "A Baltimore Jail Scandal Aided by Union Politics," *Washington Post*, May 6, 2013; Charles Lane, "Baltimore Behind Bars," *City Journal*, spring 2014.

84 **Law Enforcement Officers Bill of Rights:** Rebecca Tan, "There's a Reason It's Hard to Discipline Police. It Starts With a Bill of Rights 47 Years Ago," *Washington Post*, August 29, 2020; Kevin Rector, "Caught Fabricating Evidence, Convicted Baltimore Police Officer Remains on Force 2½ Years Later," *Baltimore Sun*, March 9, 2020; Jim Hummel, "A Pivot on Police Discipline in Rhode Island? How Officers' Bill of Rights Might Change," *Providence Journal*, March 10, 2022.

85 **Civilian oversight boards:** Nicole Dungca and Jenn Abelson, "When Communities Try to Hold Police Accountable, Law Enforcement Fights Back," *Washington Post*, April 27, 2021.

86 **40 percent of the total California state general fund:** See, e.g., Lawrence O. Picus, "An Update on California School Finance 1992–93: What Does the Future Hold?" *Journal of Education Finance* 18 (1992).

86 **a full seven percentage points:** 7 percent of the $227 billion budgeted for 2022–2023. California State Budget 2022–2023: May Revision, State of California (May 2022).

87 **"ensure stability [and take] school financing out of politics":** Lionel Chan, "Full State Funding: The Risks for Public Education," American Education Research Association (1997).

87 **increasing teachers' salaries:** Douglas Shuit, "Proposition 98: School Funding Plan: Public Employees Split With Teachers Over School Funds Measure," *Los Angeles Times* (September 16, 1988).

87 **among the highest paid:** For instance, according to a report from the NEA, California teachers have the fourth-highest starting salaries in the U.S. "NEA 2020–2021 Teacher Salary Benchmark Report," National Education Association (April 2022).

87 **the bottom quartile:** *U.S. News & World Report* ranks California public schools fortieth in the nation. "Pre-K-12 Rankings," *U.S. News & World Report* (2022).

87   **"both Washington State and Maine":** Daniel DiSalvo, *Government Against Itself: Public Union Power and Its Consequences* (New York: Oxford University Press, 2015), 110.

87   **public employee unions led a $28 million:** DiSalvo, *Government Against Itself*, 108.

87   **the New Jersey teachers unions:** Mike Lilley, "Money Equals Power: How the NJEA Dominates New Jersey Politics," Sunlight Policy Center of New Jersey, June 10, 2019, 5; see also Michael Lilley, "New Jersey Public Unions, Ascendant," *City Journal*, November 16, 2017.

87   **Andrew Cuomo faced a budget shortfall:** Associated Press, "Gov.-Elect Andrew Cuomo Warns of Tough Choices in New York's Future," November 22, 2010.

88   **Public unions in Illinois:** Illinois Senate, Senate Joint Resolution, Constitutional Amendment Number 11, 102nd General Assembly, (2022).

88   **Sixth graders in the poorest district:** Jonathan Chait, "Unlearning an Answer," *New York*, January 5, 2021.

89   **Economist Thomas Sowell reviews recent data:** Thomas Sowell, *Charter Schools and Their Enemies* (New York: Basic Books, 2020), 103–119.

89   **Success Academy 2 in Harlem:** "Success Academy Charter School, Harlem-2 Ranking," SchoolDigger.com (October 28, 2021); "P.S. 30 Hernandez/Hughes Ranking," SchoolDigger.com (October 28, 2021).

89   **"The Harlem Success teachers' contract":** Steven Brill, *Class Warfare: Inside the Fight to Fix America's Schools* (New York: Simon & Schuster, 2012), 14.

90   **"these schools are producing spectacular gains":** Chait, "Unlearning an Answer."

90   **Another union technique:** Sowell, Charter Schools and Their Enemies, 40–45.

91   **"organized the single largest volunteer phone bank":** Michael T. Hartney, *How Policies Make Interest Groups: Governments, Unions, and American Education* (Chicago: University of Chicago Press, 2022), 20.

91   **the teachers unions spent $21 million:** DiSalvo, *Government Against Itself*, 107.

91   **To defeat a proposal for vouchers in Utah:** Terry M. Moe, *Special Interest: Teachers Unions and America's Public Schools* (Washington, DC: Brookings Institution Press, 2011), 298.

91   **"Education is just one path toward a stronger community":** Andre M. Perry, "The Attack on Bad Teacher Tenure Laws Is Actual-

ly an Attack on Black Professionals," *Washington Post*, August 28, 2014, quoted by Jonathan Chait in "Why Do Teacher Unions Hate Eva Moskowitz?" *New York*, September 5, 2014.

91 **"We don't need to swap out":** Chait, "Why Do Teacher Unions Hate Eva Moskowitz?"

92 **"There is no aspect of state government operations":** DiSalvo, Government Against Itself, 113.

92 **"In the dozen years":** Chait, "Unlearning an Answer."

93 **"I am not a charter-school fan":** Chait, "Unlearning an Answer."

93 **President Biden proposed new regulations:** George F. Will, "Biden Has a Tawdry New Scheme to Cripple Charter Schools," *Washington Post*, April 22, 2022. See also editorial, "A Case of Charter School Sabotage," *Wall Street Journal*, March 27, 2022.

Chapter 8: Not Reformable: The Stranglehold of Public Employee Political Power

95 **Tocqueville:** Alexis de Tocqueville, *Democracy in America*, ed. Phillips Bradley (New York: Vintage 1990) 2:142.

97 **"A new mayor or governor":** Daniel DiSalvo, *Government Against Itself: Public Union Power and Its Consequences* (New York: Oxford University Press, 2015), 188.

97 **"outdated, inefficient and expensive 'past practices'":** Terry O'Neil and E. J. McMahon, "Taylor Made," Empire Center (May 2018), p. 18.

97 **When the Long Island Railroad:** Author interview with former Long Island Railroad official, June 2022.

97 **an impasse over a new agreement:** Brian J. Malloy, *Binding Interest Arbitration in the Public Sector: A "New" Proposal for California and Beyond*, 55 *Hastings L. J.* 245 (2003).

98 **In New York State:** New York State Civil Service Law, Article 14 § 209-a.

98 **Rhode Island:** 28 R.I. Gen. Laws Ann. § 28-9.3-12 (West); 28 R.I. Gen. Laws Ann. § 28-9.4-13 (West).

98 **far more onerous:** Under New Jersey corporate law, directors must be elected annually, and any shareholder can nominate directors. There are also explicit provisions for removal. N.J. Stat. Sec 14A:6-6. To get on the ballot for most political offices, a citizen need only secure signatures from one hundred qualified voters. N.J. Stat. Sec 19:23–8.

98   **The National Treasury Employees Union:** Author interview with Chad Hooper, May 2022. Making it difficult to resign appears to be standard practice. See Elizabeth Stelle and Nathan Benefield, "Why Pennsylvania Needs Wisconsin-Style Government Union Reform," Commonwealth Foundation, February 2022, p. 7.

98   **Some of the most significant restrictions:** See, e.g., N.J. Admin. Code § 4A:8-2.4 (establishing seniority rights for state employees); See O'Neil and McMahon, "Taylor Made," endnote 5: "Various New York State laws other than the Taylor Law guarantee additional benefits for public employees, including: paid military leave; limits on suspensions without pay for almost all government workers; limits on the number of hours police officers can work in the 'open air,' on a daily and weekly basis; the maximum number of hours firefighters can work; the number of holidays and vacation days to which police and firefighters are entitled; the maximum number of consecutive hours teachers may work; the minimum number of sick leave days for teachers; maximum sick leave accumulations for teachers; and terminal leave calculations for teachers based on accumulated sick days."

99   **"When then New York governor George Pataki":** DiSalvo, *Government Against Itself*, 188–89.

99   **"from somewhat sleepy organizations":** Richard D. Kahlenberg, "The History of Collective Bargaining Among Teachers," in Jane Hannaway and Andrew J. Rotherham, *Collective Bargaining in Education* (Cambridge, Massachusetts: Harvard Education Press, 2006), 7.

100   **Terry Moe found that:** Daniel DiSalvo, *Government Against Itself*, (Oxford, UK: Oxford University Press, 2015), 60, (citing Terry Moe, *Special Interest: Teachers Unions and America's Public Schools*, [Washington, DC, Brookings Institution: 2011] 292–93).

100   **Total reported public union spending:** See "Public Sector Unions," "Summary," "Contribution Trends, 1990–2022," OpenSecrets.org, https://www.opensecrets.org/industries/indus.php?ind=P04.

100   **Public unions receive:** $700 is a conservative figure. Annual dues for public sector unions are frequently in excess of this (e.g., New Jersey Education Association [NJEA]: $999, California Teachers Association [CTA]: $1,170). "NJEA Membership Categories/Dues," NJEA, https://www.njea.org/njea-membership-categories-dues/; "Membership Dues Structure 2020–2021," CTA, https://www.nctq.org/dms-View/SJTA-Dues-2020-21.

100   **Direct contributions and payments to candidates and PACs:** Daniel DiSalvo, *Government Against Itself*, 72–80.

101 **"58 percent of total operational expenditures":** Mike Lilley, "Follow the Money: What the NJEA Really Spends on Politics" (Sunlight Policy Center, June 2019), 26. See also Mike Lilley, "Follow the Money: The Real Money Behind the New Jersey Education Association's Political Clout," American Enterprise Institute (October 2017), 7.

101 **sixty-five lawyers helping union members:** "DC 37 Municipal Employees Legal Services," District Council 37 (accessed June 17, 2022), https://www.dc37.net/benefits/MELS.

101 **about $1.1 billion by New York City:** Government not only funds these supplemental benefits but also pays for union overhead in administering them. The balkanization of these benefits among ninety-one different funds in New York City is massively inefficient, the Citizens Budget Commission found. "Union Administered Benefit Funds: Getting More Out of a Billion Dollar Taxpayer Contribution," Citizens Budget Commission (February 8, 2018).

102 **"About 10 percent of delegates":** Daniel DiSalvo and Michael Hartney, "Teachers Unions in the Post-Janus World," *Education Next,* 20(4), 46–54.

102 **"The California Correctional Peace Officers Association":** DiSalvo, *Government Against Itself,* 71.

103 **"We elect our bosses":** American Federation of State, County, and Municipal Employees, "Questions & Answers About AFSCME," (2017), https://www.afscme.org/about/AFSCME-WMAH-QA-Booklet.pdf; DiSalvo, *Government Against Itself,* 19.

103 **In many states:** Michael T. Hartney, *How Policies Make Interest Groups: Governments, Unions, and American Education* (Chicago: University of Chicago Press, 2022), 145.

103 **"Electing Your Own Employer":** Moe, *Special Interest,* 113.

103 **70 percent of union-endorsed school board candidates win:** Hartney, *How Policies Make Interest Groups,* 147–48.

104 **"In an awesome display of raw political power":** Moe, *Special Interest,* 226.

104 **"put the hard sell on":** Mike DeBonis, "As Next D.C. Mayor, Gray Will Have to Deal With Debt to Unions," *Washington Post,* November 17, 2010.

105 **The American Federation of Teachers:** Ben Smith, "Teachers Union Helped Unseat Fenty," *Politico,* September 15, 2010.

105 **The unions built an astonishing war chest:** DiSalvo, *Government Against Itself*, 69.

106 **They organized a massive demonstration:** James B. Kelleher, "Up to 100,000 Protest Wisconsin Law Curbing Unions," Reuters (March 12, 2011).

106 **Protests of thousands of union employees:** Abby Sewell, "Protesters Out in Force Nationwide to Oppose Wisconsin's Anti-Union Bill," *Los Angeles Times* (February 26, 2011).

106 **To prevent a vote on the law:** NPR Staff, "Wisconsin Democrats Flee to Prevent Vote on Union Bill," National Public Radio (February 17, 2011).

106 **marshaled $18 million:** Peter Whoriskey and Dan Balz, "Wisconsin Gov. Scott Walker's Victory Deals Blow to Unions," *Washington Post*, June 6, 2012. See also DiSalvo, *Government Against Itself*, 68–71.

107 **"the special prosecutor's legal theory":** Adam B. Lerner, "Wisconsin Supreme Court Rules Walker Didn't Violate Campaign Finance Laws," *Politico* (July 16, 2015).

107 **employed seventeen lobbyists:** Shawn Johnson, "A Decade After Act 10, It's a Different World for Wisconsin Unions," Wisconsin Public Radio (February 21, 2021).

107 **By most accounts:** See Stelle and Nathan Benefield, *Why Pennsylvania Needs*, 7–12.

107 **he disguised his intention:** After Walker was elected, the unions were willing to compromise on pension and health-care benefits but would not give in on collective bargaining. They argued that it was unfair to reform collective bargaining because Walker had not signaled during his campaign that he planned to overhaul collective bargaining. See William Finnegan, "The Storm," *The New Yorker*, February 27, 2012.

108 **"succeed in raising school budgets":** Caroline Hoxby, "How Teachers Unions Affect Education Production," *Qu. J. of Economics*, vol. 111 (August 1996), pp. 671–718.

108 **Series of reports by Michael Lilley:** The following descriptions of NJEA political activity are taken from these reports. Mike Lilley, "Follow the Money" (Sunlight Policy Center, June 3, 2019); "Follow the Money" (American Enterprise Institute, October 2017); "'And You Will Pay'" (American Enterprise Institute, October 2017); "Money Equals Power" (Sunlight Policy Center, June 10, 2019); "Councilman Spiller, Mayor Spiller, Governor Spiller?" (Sunlight Policy Center, April 20, 2020); and "Blue Jersey" (Sunlight Policy Center, October 20, 2021).

112 **$10.5 million to the pro-Murphy New Direction New Jer-sey:** Matt Arco, "Names of Donors to Pro-Murphy Group Finally Revealed," NJ.com, September 12, 2019; "New Direction New Jersey Voluntarily Releases Donor List for the Second Year in a Row," *Insider NJ*, December 23, 2020. See also Ashley Balcerzak and Charles Stile, "NJEA Donates $750,000 to Another Political Dark Money Group Tied to Phil Murphy," NorthJersey.com, June 22, 2022.

114 **"They'd like to take over":** Dana Goldstein, "Chicago Mayor Lori Lightfoot on What She Learned From Battling the Teachers' Union," *New York Times*, February 14, 2021.

Chapter 9: What Were They Thinking?

115 **"The spirit of distrust of authority":** Robert Kagan, "Adversarial Legalism and American Government," 10 *Journal of Policy Analysis & Management* 369, 375 (1991).

116 **The 1966 Taylor Report:** Governor's Committee on Public Employee Relations, Final Report, March 31, 1966, 11–12, 20, 39, 46.

117 **Expert reports were also commissioned:** Russell A. Smith, "State and Local Advisory Reports on Public Employment Labor Legislation: A Comparative Analysis," 67 *Mich. L. Rev.* 891, 907 (1969).

118 **Yale Law labor expert Clyde Summers:** Clyde W. Summers, "Bargaining in the Government's Business," 18 *U Tol. L. Rev.* 265, 272–73 (1987). Summers's 1987 summary of justifications and limits of public bargaining reflected ideas he had advocated during the early years of public bargaining. See Summers, "Public Employee Bargaining," 83 *Yale L. J.* 1156 (1974); Summers, "Public Sector Bargaining," 44 *U. Cin. L. Rev.* 769 (1975).

118 **"wrong in principle":** Summers, "Bargaining in the Government's Business," 289.

119 **Professor Summers came up with two justifications:** Summers, "Bargaining in the Government's Business," 268–72.

119 **"rights ... similar to those accorded in the private sector":** Smith, "State and Local Advisory Reports," 896.

119 **"The danger to [the American political]":** Harry Wellington and Ralph Winter, "Structuring Collective Bargaining in Public Employment," 79 *Yale L. J.* 805, 810 (1970).

120 **Instead of labor peace:** Theodore W. Kheel, "Strikes and Public Employment," 67 *Mich. L. Rev.* 931, 935–36 (1969).

121 **"a power relationship":** Petro, "Sovereignty," 85.

122 **"Whenever a question arises":** Petro, "Sovereignty," 47.

122 **"forc[ing] everyone to work for it":** Petro, "Sovereignty," 75.

122 **"amounts to a voluntary forfeiture":** Petro, "Sovereignty," 81.

123 **"[Compulsory bargaining has] the potential":** Kurt Hanslowe, *The Emerging Law of Labor Relations in Public Employment* (Ithaca, New York: New York School of Industrial and Labor Relations at Cornell University, 1967), quoted in Petro at 127

124 **"The employer is the whole people":** Franklin D. Roosevelt to Luther C. Steward, August 16, 1937, from the American Presidency Project.

SECTION III: PUBLIC EMPLOYEE CONTROLS ARE UNCONSTITUTIONAL

125 **"In framing a government":** James Madison, "Federalist no. 51," in Alexander Hamilton, John Jay, and James Madison, *The Federalist Papers,* (Project Gutenberg Etext, 1998).

127 **"The power of governing":** Stone v. Mississippi, 101 U.S. 814 (1880).

127 **"nondelegation principle":** John Locke, *Second Treatise of Government* (Oxford, UK: Oxford University Press: 2016), 72.

128 **"We have the power":** Sylvester Petro, "Sovereignty and Compulsory Public Sector Bargaining," *Wake Forest Law Review* 10, no. 1 (March 1974), 122.

128 **"Let a State be considered":** Chisholm v. Georgia, 2 U.S. 419 (1793), 455.

128 **"virtually total control":** Editorial Board, "Total Control by U.F.T.?" *New York Times* (July 3, 1972).

128 **"a power relationship":** Edwin Vieira Jr., "Are Public Sector Unions Special Interest Political Parties?" 27 *DePaul Law Review* 293 (1978), 365.

129 **"the whole people":** Franklin D. Roosevelt, "Letter on the Resolution of Federal Employees Against Strikes in Federal Service," (August 16, 1937).

129 **"The collective agreement":** Clyde Summers, "Bargaining in the Government's Business: Principles and Politics," *Toledo Law Review* 18 (1987), 266.

129 **"Under our form of government":** City of Springfield v. Clouse, 206 S.W.2d 539 (1947), 545.

130 **"write collective bargaining agreements":** See, e.g., City of Buffalo v. Rinaldo, 41 N.Y. 2d 764 (1977).

130 **"There is serious doubt":** "Governor's Committee on Public Employee Relations: Final Report," (March 31, 1966), 46.

130 **"Arbitrators are seldom equipped":** Derek Bok and John Dunlop, *Labor and the American Community*, (New York, Simon & Schuster: 1970), 337.

131 **In the 1973 *Letter Carriers* case:** United States Civil Service Commission v. National Association of Letter Carriers, 413 U.S. 548 (1973).

133 **In the recent *Janus* and *Knox* decisions:** Janus v. American Federation of State, County, and Municipal Employees, 138 S. Ct. 2448 (2018), and Knox v. Service Employees International Union, 567 U.S. 298 (2012).

Chapter 10: Restore Executive Power under Article II

135 **"Certain powers":** James Madison, "Original Notes on Debates in the Congress of Confederation," (June 1, 1787).

135 **The Supreme Court on many occasions:** See, e.g., Ex parte Hennen, 38 U.S. 230 (1839); Parsons v. United States, 167 U.S. 324 (1897); Humphrey's Executor v. United States, 295 U.S. 602 (1935); Buckley v. Valeo, 424 U.S. 1 (1976); Myers v. United States, 272 U.S. 52 (1926); Bowsher v. Synar, 478 U.S. 714 (1986); Morrison v. Olson, 487 U.S. 654 (1988); Edmond v. United States, 520 U.S. 651 (1997); Free Enterprise Fund v. Public Company Accounting Oversight Board, 561 U.S. 477 (2010); and Lucia v. S.E.C., 585 U.S. ___ (2018).

135 **Civil Service Reform Act of 1978:** Pub. L. 95–454, 92 Stat. 1111 (codified as amended in scattered sections of 5 U.S.C.).

136 **25 percent of federal employees:** Bureau of Labor Statistics, "Union Members—2021" (January 20, 2022).

136 **an independent Impasses Panel:** 5 U.S.C. § 7119(c).

136 **the Impasses Panel required:** In the Matter of Department of Veterans Affairs and Local 200 United, Service Employees International Union, "Arbitrator's Opinion and Decision," Case No. 15 FSIP 28 (September 5, 2015).

136 **More federal employees:** See, e.g., Dennis Cauchon, "Some Federal Workers More Likely to Die Than Lose Jobs," *USA Today* (July 19, 2011).

136 **EPA employee:** See discussion in Introduction. See also, e.g., Charles S. Clark, "Lawmakers Wonder 'How Much Porn' It Takes to Fire an EPA Employee," *Government Executive* (May 8, 2014).

136 **The head of the VA hospital:** Steven Brill, *Tailspin: The People and Forces Behind America's Fifty-Year Fall—and Those Fighting to Reverse It* (New York: Knopf, 2018), 206.

136 **an employee who systematically denied benefits:** Author interview with Chad Hooper, May 2022.

137 **"fully successful":** Memorandum from Robert Goldenkoff, director of strategic issues, Government Accountability Office, to Ron Johnson, chairman, Senate Committee on Homeland Security and Governmental Affairs (May 9, 2016), 5.

137 **an office move at the Department of Energy:** Author interview with Bill Valdez, May 2022.

137 **The National Treasury Employees Union agreement:** Author interview with Chad Hooper, May 2022. See Internal Revenue Service and National Treasury Employees Union, 2019 National Agreement, 161.

137 **the original Volcker National Commission on the Public Service:** National Commission on Public Service, *Leadership for America: Rebuilding the Public Service*, (1989), 3, 45.

138 **The second Volcker Commission:** National Commission on Public Service, *Urgent Business for America: Revitalizing the Federal Government for the 21st Century* (2003), 12.

138 **"I found that most people":** Author interview with Chad Hooper, June 2022.

138 **The Partnership for Public Service in 2014:** Partnership for Public Service, "Building the Enterprise: A New Civil Service Framework" (April 1, 2014), 7.

138 **"It should not require":** Jason Briefel, email message to the author, June 9, 2022.

139 **"as effectively and efficiently as possible":** Connick v. Myers, 461 U.S. 138 (1983).

139 **"Government employers, like private employers":** Garcetti v. Ceballos, 547 U.S. 410 (2006), 418.

139 **"The Constitution that makes the President accountable":** Free Enterprise Fund v. Public Company Accounting Oversight Board, 561 U.S. 477, 130 S. Ct. 3138 (2010), 3164.

140 **"examination of witnesses, trial, or hearing":** Arnett v. Kennedy, 416 U.S. 134 (1974) (quoting the Lloyd-LaFollette Act).

140 **Humphrey's Executor:** Humphrey's Executor v. United States, 295 U.S. 602 (1935), 629. The court held that "whether the power of the President to remove an officer shall prevail over the authority of Congress ... will depend upon the character of the office." Id, p. 631.

140 **In those situations:** There are also a group of due process cases from the 1970s, not addressing Article II, which treat public jobs in certain situations as a property right that cannot be removed except by due process. As if suffering from constitutional amnesia, those cases do not address Article II. See, e.g., Board of Regents of States Colleges v. Roth, 408 U.S. 564 (1972); Perry v. Sindermann, 408 U.S. 593 (1972). More recent cases about public employees' rights revert to the constitutional imperative for executive power.

Chapter 11: Public Union Controls Undermine Democratic Governance

141 **"It is one of the most prominent features of the Constitution":** James Madison, speech in Congress on the Removal Power, May 19, 1789, in *Writings* (Library of America: 1999), 435.

142 **as described by James Madison in Federalist 39:** James Madison, "Federalist no. 39," in Alexander Hamilton, John Jay, and James Madison, *The Federalist Papers,* (Project Gutenberg Etext, 1998). Referring to the Constitution's prohibition of titles of nobility in Article I, section 9 ("No Title of Nobility shall be granted by the United States"), Madison concludes that the guarantee of a republican form of government in the states will thus prevent any form of government not accountable to "the great body of society": "Could any further proof be required of the republican complexion of this system, the most decisive one might be found in its absolute prohibition of titles of nobility, both under the federal and the State governments; and in its express guaranty of the republican form to each of the latter."

143 **"Lincoln reasoned that if a state may secede":** William M. Wiecek, *The Guarantee Clause of the U.S. Constitution* (Ithaca, New York: Cornell University Press, 1972), 171.

143 **Abolitionists had long invoked:** Wiecek, *The Guarantee Clause,* 133–65.

144 **in an 1849 case:** Luther v. Borden, 48 U.S. 1 (1849). Professor Louise Weinberg argues that Taney's conclusion that the Guarantee Clause is nonjusticiable is motivated by Taney's desire to avoid letting abolitionists and antislavery advocates invoke the Guarantee Clause to try to get a ruling declaring slavery unconstitutional. Louise Weinberg, "Luther v Borden; A Taney Court Mystery Solved," 37 *Pace L. Rev.* 700, 758 (2017).

144 **In a 1912 case:** Pacific States Telephone and Telegraph Company v. Oregon, 223 U.S. 118 (1912).

144 **In *Baker v. Carr:*** Baker v. Carr, 369 U.S. 186 (1962), 218.

144 **Recent political questions:** See, e.g., Rucho v. Common Cause, 139 S. Ct. 2484 (2019).

145 **"The fiscal problems of the City":** Rinaldo, 41 N.Y. 2d 764, 767.

146 **"Private arbitration of public-sector disputes":** Petro, "Sovereignty," 104.

146 **"a government which derives":** James Madison, "Federalist no. 39," in Alexander Hamilton, John Jay, and James Madison, *The Federalist Papers,* (Project Gutenberg Etext, 1998).

Chapter 12: Public Service Is a Public Trust, not a Political Party

147 **"Most evil is done":** Hannah Arendt, *The Life of the Mind* (New York: Harcourt Inc., 1977), 180.

148 ***"Public service is a public trust":*** 5 C.F.R. § 2635.101(a).

148 **"obligation to put the public's interest":** Hana Callaghan, "Trusting a Trust: What Does the Duty to Avoid Conflicts of Interest Demand?" Santa Clara University, Markkulla Center for Applied Ethics, April 5, 2017.

148 **Fiduciary duty:** See discussion in David L. Ponet and Ethan J. Lieb, "Fiduciary Law's Lessons for Deliberative Democracy," *Boston University Law Review* 91 (2013), 1256–60: "Because fiduciaries are difficult to monitor and have wide access to power over beneficiary resources and assets, fiduciaries are under rigorous obligations that ensure compliance with their role responsibilities."

149 **"[The policeman is] entirely responsible":** Gardner v. Broderick, 392 U.S. 273 (1968), 277.

149 **refused to let police join his union:** See, e.g., Steven Greenhouse, "How Police Unions Enable and Conceal Abuses of Power," *The New Yorker,* June 18, 2020.

149 **"represent his own personal interests":** Massachusetts Office of the Inspector General, "Summary of the Conflict of Interest Law for State Employees," Section IV(b) (last revised May 10, 2013).

150 **the Supreme Court has repeatedly held:** See, e.g., Garcetti, 547 U.S. 410; Connick v. Myers, 461 U.S. 138 (1983); Pickering v. Board of Education, 391 U.S. 536 (1968).

151 **"It seems fundamental":** Letter Carriers, 413 U.S. 548, 565.

151 **"The political orientation of public-sector unions":** Petro, "Sovereignty," 86.

152 **In the 2012 *Knox* case:** Knox, 567 U.S. 298.

152 **"increasing use of campaign contributions":** R. Theodore Clark Jr., "Politics and Public Employee Unionism: Some Recommendations for an Emerging Problem," 44 *U. Cin. L. Rev.* 680, 684 (1975).

152 **Prior to collective bargaining:** See Lorraine M. McDonnell, "The Internal Politics of the NEA." *The Phi Delta Kappan* 58, no. 2 (1976): 185–201: "For over 100 years the National Education Association, the nation's oldest and largest teacher organization, emphasized the professional unity of all educators and the consensual relationships that should exist between the teaching profession and the governing bodies of public education. Yet in less than 10 years these organizational goals were radically changed. Instead of the concept of professional unity, the conflicts of interest that exist between classroom teachers and school administrators were emphasized. School boards were regarded as potential adversaries, and the NEA actively promoted the rights of teachers to bargain collectively."

152 **Over 75 percent of public employees in Denmark and Canada:** Canada: interview by author with Canadian labor lawyer Steven Barrett, May 2022; Denmark: interview by author with Sigge Winther Nielsen, June 2022.

153 **in the 2018 *Janus* case:** Janus, 585 U.S. ___ (2018).

156 **"There are limits on the amount of stress":** Kurt Hanslowe, *The Emerging Law of Labor Relations in Public Employment* (Ithaca, New York: New York School of Industrial and Labor Relations at Cornell University, 1967), 115–16.

Chapter 13: Abolish the Union Spoils System

157 **"We are determined to respect everyone":** Christopher Lasch, *The Revolt of the Elites* (New York: W.W. Norton, 1996), 80,107.

157 **"A Nation at Risk":** A Nation at Risk (U.S. Government Printing Office, 1983).

157 **a follow-up report:** Strong American Schools, "A Stagnant Nation" (2008).

158 **As Michael Hartney explains:** Michael T. Hartney, *How Policies Make Interest Groups: Governments, Unions, and American Education* (Chicago: University of Chicago Press, 2022), 104–05.

159 **"They are ... active at every level of political activity—lobbying":** Sylvester Petro, "Sovereignty and Compulsory Public Sector Bargaining," *Wake Forest Law Review* 10, no. 1 (March 1974), 88.

160   **the Centers for Disease Control:** See discussion in Philip K. How-
       ard, *Try Common Sense: Replacing the Failed Ideologies of Right and Left* (New
       York: W. W. Norton, 2019), 97.

160   **"Civil servants bear special responsibilities":** Christoph Dem-
       mke, "Are Civil Servants Different Because They Are Civil Servants,"
       European Institute of Public Administration, Sec. 5.2.1 (June 2005).

161   **The 1989 Volcker Commission:** The National Commission on the
       Public Service, Leadership for America, 45 (1989).

161   **"code of silence":** See, e.g., Dhammika Dharmapala, Richard H.
       McAdams, and John Rappaport, "Collective Bargaining Rights and
       Police Misconduct: Evidence from Florida," *The Journal of Law, Econom-
       ics, and Organization* 38 (March 2022).

161   **Good teachers quit:** Jason E. Lane, "Teachers Are Quitting in
       Droves," *The Hill*, May 7, 2022.

161   **"walk around [the capitol] like they're God":** Allysia Finley,
       "Gloria Romero: The Trials of a Democratic Reformer," *Wall Street
       Journal*, August 31, 2012.

161   **twenty-seventh in World Bank ratings:** "Government Effective-
       ness—Country Rankings," TheGlobalEconomy.com.

161   **Public trust is also low:** OECD perceptions of corruption. OECD,
       "Public Integrity: A Strategy Against Corruption," 2.

162   **"Government is competent":** Franklin D. Roosevelt, "Second
       Inaugural Address," speech, Washington, DC, 1937, "The Ava-
       lon Project: Documents in Law, History and Diplomacy," Yale Law
       School Avalon Project.

162   **"Culture eats strategy":** The Management Centre, "Transform-
       ing Results by Changing Beliefs and Behaviours," https://www.man-
       agement-centre.co.uk/management-consultancy/culture-eats-strate-
       gy-for-breakfast/.

162   **"The key is pride":** David Osborne and Peter Plastrik, *Banishing Bu-
       reaucracy* (New York: Basic Books, 1997), Sec VI, 108.

162   **"No one has a greater asset":** ed. Pauline Graham, *Mary Parker Fol-
       lett, Prophet of Management* (Washington, DC: Beard Books, 2003), 126.

162   **"far-reaching changes":** National Commission on Public Service,
       Urgent Business for America (January 2003), 13.

163   **"Thou shalt not make a mistake":** Robert D. Behn, "Creating an
       Innovative Organization," 27 *State and Local Government Review* No. 3
       (Fall 1995).

163 **"the best policy is to give people one chance":** Osborne and Plastrik, *Banishing Bureaucracy*, Sec VI, 39–40.

163 **"You don't have to fire all the resisters":** Osborne and Plastrik, *Banishing Bureaucracy*, 40.

Acknowledgments

This book grew out of a project for a Common Good white paper. Common Good executive director Matt Brown and head of research Andy Park threw themselves into it and were indispensable. Consultant Seth Karecha and law intern Charles Ziscovici were energetic and effective members of the core team. Their dedication, diligence, and long hours demonstrated a commitment to professionalism that made this project possible. Communications adviser Henry Miller was a thoughtful reader of many drafts. Ron Faucheux advised on general approach. Donna Thompson is indefatigable and effective in outreach. Ruth Mary Giverin keeps the trains at Common Good running on time.

Long discussions with Common Good supporter and former law colleague Richard Bartlett helped shape my thinking on the duties of public employees and the differences between trade unions and public employee unions. My friend and neighbor Sean Brady read late drafts and made valuable suggestions, especially about the constitutional arguments. David Johnson provided fresh eyes on late drafts.

Political scientist Daniel DiSalvo was a key adviser. E. J. McMahon and Terry O'Neil provided key insights on public unions in New York and labor law and were critical readers. Public management guru David Osborne was a resource and thoughtful reader. Michael Lilley's investigative work in New Jersey was an invaluable resource, and Mike was very helpful in guiding me through it.

Leading experts were generous in reading drafts and suggesting leads. E. Donald Elliott was an invaluable resource as the project unfolded and introduced Charles Ziscovici to the project. Law professors Philip Bobbitt, Julia Mahoney, and James Maxeiner were constitutional sounding boards and thoughtful readers. Andrew Rein at the Citizens Budget Commission was generous with his time and research. Judge Randall Shepard sent his law school notes on the Guarantee Clause. Paul Light, Philip Hamburger, and Peter Schuck provided early feedback.

Many prominent citizens and academics were helpful in offering their perspectives and tracking down leads. In public finance, Eugene Steuerle and my Covington & Burling colleagues Richard Shea and Jack Lund; in education, Alan Bersin, Rick Hess, and Paul Hill; in law, Mary Ann Glendon, Richard Pildes, Ross Sandler, and David Schoenbrod; for federal civil service, Jason Briefel, Chad Hooper, and Mark Valdez; in Canada, Steven Barrett and Donald Ross; in the UK, Lord Francis Maude; in Germany, Michael zu Loewenstein; in Denmark, Sigge Nielsen, Christian Madsbjerg and Steen Lassen; for Kentucky education, Clay Ford, David Jones,

Kate McAnelly, Harvie Wilkinson, and Stuart Silberman; in New York, Pat Foye, Richard Kahan, Ernie Oliveri, Kathy Wylde, and a few officials who would prefer not to be named; in Connecticut, Red Jahncke; in Illinois, Mailee Smith of Illinois Policy Institute. Economist Mark Zupan provided a unique perspective. Conrad Scott and Tyler Jankauskas at Covington were thoughtful sounding boards. Law intern Patrick Cazalet combed administrative decisions.

None of this would be possible without the generous support of Common Good directors. Tony Kiser and Scott Smith served double duty as advisers as well as supporters. John Messervey and Alan Siegel are key advisers. Long-time Common Good supporter Fritz Hobbs is a sounding board.

The publishing team was organized brilliantly on short notice by Arthur Klebanoff at Rodin Books and included David Wilk at Booktrix and Rodin marketing head Michelle Weyenberg. Ben Riley provided helpful editorial advice. Blair Fitzgibbon is a key communications adviser.

Alexandra Cushing Howard was ever encouraging and kept the home fires burning. Thank you all.